THE BRIDGE

Stories of the Church Body Becoming the Living Proof of a Loving God in its Hurting Urban Neighborhood

J. Nelson Warner

CROSSBOOKS
PUBLISHING

CrossBooks™
A Division of LifeWay
One LifeWay Plaza
Nashville, TN 37234
www.crossbooks.com
Phone: 1-866-768-9010

First published by CrossBooks 11/25/14

ISBN: 978-1-4627-5596-7 (sc)
ISBN: 978-1-4627-5597-4 (hc)
ISBN: 978-1-4627-5595-0 (e)

Library of Congress Control Number: 2014921080

Printed in the United States of America.

This book is printed on acid-free paper.

Bridge Ministry of Acadiana, Inc.
512 North University Ave.
Lafayette, Louisiana 70501
337.235.5565
www.bridgeacadiana.com
Jennifer Reynaud, Executive director
P.O. Box 62029, Lafayette, 70596

Vision:

To relationally empower lives through spiritual transformation, education, and neighborhood revitalization.

Mission:

Bridge Ministry is an interdenominational Christian holistic ministry called to:

1) provide relationship-based programs which empower the under-resourced and
2) mobilize Christians to social responsibility.

Contents

Acknowledgements xi
Foreword xvi
River Babies 1
SENT 5
Amachi 11
Kids Say The Darndest Things! 14
The Simplest Of Gifts 17
A Boy Was Born 21
The Blue Trashcans 26
The Rule Of Detachment 28
It Works 31
Exchanging Pronouns 33
Forgiveness 35
An Admired Boy 37
Church Decline And Ascent 40
Economics 101 46
Higher Expectations 49
Take It With A Smile! 53
It Doesn't Feel Good 56
Thanking All Fathers 59
The Power Of Friendship 64
New Caring, New Thinking, New Behavior 67
Flying Lesson 70
God's Pathway 73
The Bridge: Past ~ Present ~ Beyond 77
Learning To Walk (And Keeping Your Balance) 80

Without Hope 82
LEARNING BY DOING 84
Heroes Of Hope 87
When Can I Come To Bridge? 90
Family Fun Day In The Park 93
An Old Man And A Boy 96
The Symphony 99
Do Good, Feel Good 102
Irritations 106
Showing God's Loving-Kindness 109
De'vante 111
Back Pack Pals 114
Our Father 119
Destiny 122
Heavy Lifting 126
The Third & Fourth Worlds 130
A Boy And A Man 134
Girl Drama 137
Grit 140
The Shaft Of Light 144
The Seeds Of Friendships 146
Joy 149
Recommended Reading List 155

Acknowledgements

At fifty years old I was sitting on top of the world. I had attained economic success, and yet something was missing deep within me. I felt my spirit was dead and needed life. Finding myself empty-at-fifty after having climbed a ladder that was leaning against the wrong wall, I began my spiritual journey towards wholeness.

In my search for greater meaning through a men's Bible study, I met Tim Osborne, Phil Judice, Keith Rodriquez, Dan Hughes, Mike Bertucci and others. Within six months of wrestling with the question of God's existence, God revealed clearly that He loved me. I had no other choice but to love Him back. That was November 9, 1999.

A few months later, Tim and my pastor, Dennis Malcolm, mentored us in the Navigators 2.7 Discipleship course. They taught us that the Holy Scriptures were alive and living. They taught us that God's primary means of speaking to us is through His word. They taught us how to develop a daily habit of spending meditative time with our Lord and His word and allow our Lord to speak directly to us.

Through the study, I learned how to teach others. Within three years, God and His Word began opening my heart and mind to God's heart and mind toward the fatherless children in our inner-city. Others at my church,

Trinity Bible Church in Lafayette, La., were also being moved and positioned by God in the same direction. We came together in our holy discontent for the under-resourced in our community.

We searched Lafayette for signs of where God was working in hopes of finding an organization to join, but we found nothing being done that seemed relevant to addressing the true roots of poverty. There were many organizations that provided fish, but we found none that taught people how to fish and eventually to own a part of the fishing pond.

Pastor Malcolm's good friend Jimmy Dorrell, a theology professor at Baylor, and pastor of the Church Under the Bridge in Waco, Texas (churchunderthebridge.org), operates Mission Waco (missionwaco.org/missionwaco), offered the biblical model for the kind of inner-city development program we wanted. Jimmy became our coach. He began teaching us how to make our faith relevant in the lives of those in our inner-city. He taught us a practical faith that begins and ends in love.

In 2002, Jimmy directed us to the Christian Community Development Association (CCDA.org). He recommended practical books of faith to read and study. He guided us in acquiring the right biblical principles of development before we began our actions. Beginning with the right principles and valuing what God values, have proven critical to success in our urban relationships and environment. With God at the helm and in bold faith, we created Bridge Ministry of Acadiana and moved into an inner-city neighborhood, as Jesus moved into our neighborhood.

In 2003, Bridge Ministry (Bridge) rented a house in

one of Lafayette's most under-resourced neighborhoods where drug trafficking, prostitution, and crime were most visible. We began going door to door to learn about our neighbor's dreams. People told us they dreamed of having safe streets and secure homes again. They dreamed of a neighborhood void of drugs and prostitution. They also dreamed of having respectful children who did well in school and beyond. Using their hopes and dreams as a guide, we began developing our multifaceted, relational, daily programs, which the neighborhood and its children readily embraced.

The Bridge became a member of the CCDA where 3,000 plus faithful urban missionaries come together every year from around the United States (and beyond) to share in a variety of practical inner-city workshops (faithshops), fellowship, and worship. The CCDA was begun by John M. Perkins of Jackson, Miss. Along with Dr. Dorrell and Dr. Perkins, we have been blessed by many other CCDA mentors, including Dr. Wayne Gordon, Glen Kehrein (deceased), Dr. Soong-Chan Rah, Dr. Amy Sherman, Mo Leverett, Lowell Noble, Mary Nelson, and Dr. Robert Lupton. It is at Jesus' feet and theirs that we are being taught how to make our faith relevant and to wholeheartedly love God, self, and our neighbors in right and meaningful ways for the King's and Kingdom's sake and glory. We thank you all.

I owe a special thanks to Robert Lupton who inspired this book through his monthly newsletters and books. I copied his model of monthly newsletter stories that comprise this book. I began to write these Bridge stories to our investors, volunteers, those praying for the ministry, friends and anyone interested in Bridge's urban journey. In appreciation to Dr. Lupton, I have included one of his monthly letters in this book. Thank you Dr. Lupton, I admire your concise writing, your talent and insights, but mostly your heart, like all the other wonderful hearts in the CCDA.

Thank you to the Bridge Board for all of your faithfulness, guidance, wisdom, and friendships. I extend a big thank you to Connie Sanders, our first Executive Director and leader. You taught me a lot. I especially thank our Executive Director, Jennifer Reynaud. Jennifer has certainly been sent by God to take Bridge to higher levels still. And a big thank-you to our Bridge Staff: Erin Greneaux, Joel Green Lee, Tony Boutte, Jennifer Bourque, Joslynn Stakes, and Toi James. We need to support and pray for our young staff that is in the urban-trenches every day. I am humbled by our staff's grace, faith, love, justice, and wisdom. The urban mission field, for many reasons, is the toughest mission field in the world, yet the harvest is most bountiful.

I also want to thank the People Helping People Neighborhood Association. I admire your strength, courage, and friendship that is active in taking back your streets from drugs and prostitution. You are a great model for our community.

A special thank you to Carol Stubbs who freely gave of her time to guide, write, proof read and encourage.

It does not take any old village to raise child, it takes a Beloved Village like Lafayette. What a great community! It is our community and churches that support the Bridge's inner city mission with prayers, volunteers, and financial support. We are most grateful to you all. Thank you.

God is gaining ground in our area, as five under-resourced neighborhoods are now served by CCDA type ministries like the Bridge.

Finally, I thank Jesus Christ for my wife, Jan. I love and respect you a bunch, gal! You are more than my better half and God's gift to me.

Foreword

At Bridge Ministry of Acadiana we see poverty as a symptom with a deeper root cause. Some people see poverty as a lack of money, or lack of education or lack of resources and it is, but there is a deeper root cause to these symptoms that must be addressed and not neglected. The root cause of poverty is due to our broken relations with God, self(s), and neighbors. These interdependent broken relationships cause a gap in the resource flow needed for human development and empowerment. These 3-Broken relationships ultimately cause physical as well as spiritual poverty.

Jesus Christ moved into our broken neighborhood here on earth to reconcile and redeem these 3-broken relationships for the Kingdom's sake. Jesus now directs us in His Greatest Commandments to love God, self(s) and neighbors with all our minds, hearts and strength. As purposed, it is in these right and caring relationships intellectual, moral, and spiritual resources are then able to flow for the edification of the Body of Christ and all mankind.

Many people ask us at Bridge Ministry of Acadiana, What does Bridge do? Before speaking about our actions, which are hopefully reflected in this book's short stories, I prefer to begin speaking about our principles.

It is critical that we establish the right principles

before we begin acting, because our principles will drive our actions. At Bridge, our thinking-caring-acting process is done within the framework of Jesus's Greatest Commandments.

Matthew 22:37-40 (NLT): You must love the Lord your God with all your heart, all your soul, and all your mind; and love your neighbor as yourself.

Within the framework of Jesus's Greatest Commandments, the Christian Community Development Association (CCDA) that Bridge Ministry of Acadiana is a member has developed eight Key Components that begin with the 3-R's of Development:

8 Key Components of Development

Relocation

Jesus Christ relocated, because the best practice of service is being in close physical relationship to the one being served. As Jesus moves into our neighborhood, we are to go and do the same. At Bridge we have humbly relocated into a specific inner-city neighborhood.

Reconciliation

Understanding that the root issues of poverty are caused by our broken relationships with God, self, neighbors, and creation, we answer God's call to lovingly reconcile these broken relationships. Inside God's Will to love, reconciliation is best done in our closest proximity to God and our neighbors.

Redemption

As Christ's Spirit works through our faith, love, righteousness, and resulting justice, God is able to redeem what has been lost of the Kingdom on earth through us. We believe that justice must include economics to reach the wholeness of shalom (Hebrew word for peace). In seeking wholeness for this under-resourced neighborhood, we will find our own wholeness.

Leadership Development

We believe that there is no success without successors who can take our place. Making leaders who are both capable and caring and able to teach others is a high priority at Bridge.

Listening to Community

Listen-Listen-Learn-Learn-Love-Love. Recognizing that our neighborhood residents know their issues better than we do, we listen and learn. When we listen, we are being respectful and loving, and where there is love, there is learning. The Bridge does not follow a "needs-based" relief approach, but follows an "asset-based" development approach, which builds on the assets already in the neighborhood. In being an asset-based mission, we see the glass half-full instead of half-empty. We believe the people on both sides of the Bridge are the solution, when they meet and become friends. At Bridge, we see our neighbors holding the key to our community's wholeness and shalom, we just need to listen-learn-love.

Church-Based

Bridge Ministry of Acadiana obediently maintains its Christ centered DNA. *God's Will be done* is His pathway to His Kingdom on earth, as it is in heaven. At Bridge the Church (capital "C") is not peripheral to the world, but the world is peripheral to the Church's grace and truth.

Wholistic Approach

The Wholistic Approach to Development focuses on the whole person. The goal is for each person to grow straight, strong, and whole—mentally, spiritually, physically, economically, and socially. The physical and spiritual are equally important, with wholeness of Christ's character being the goal. After all, whole people, who are both capable and caring, make up whole families, who make up whole neighborhoods and whole communities.

Empowerment/Development (not Relief)

There are basically two types of organizations. "Relief" is short term, but can cause dependency if continued for too long. When "Development" begins, relief should cease. Development is the long-term daily walk with another that develops capable and caring people on both sides. Development does not do "for," but does "with," embracing each other's struggles, not fixing them. Our dream for our inner cities is in development and empowerment, not relief. After short term relief, human dignity demands long term development and empowerment. After all, justice must end in the economics of self-sufficiency.

These are CCDA's "8 Key components of Development" that we value at Bridge Ministry of Acadiana. These eight keys are the underlying principles that lead us into caring, right and just actions. These keys, working within the framework of Jesus' Greatest Commandments, form the developmental guideposts for our many programs and actions at Bridge Ministry of Acadiana. Thus, Bridge's development mission is highly relational and multifaceted.

As you read the following stories, please reflect on our Christian principles that guide our actions in our inner-city of Lafayette.

<u>Bridge's Philosophy</u>:

Go to the people,
Live among them,
Learn from them,
Love them,
Start with what they know,
Build with what they have,
But with the best of leaders,
When their task is done,
The people will remark:
"We have done it ourselves!"

For more information about Bridge Ministry of Acadiana go to http://www.bridgeacadiana.com

RIVER BABIES

(Modified from Kip Tiernan's original story)

Once upon a time there was a small church on the edge of a river just upstream from a dangerous waterfall. The church people there were happy and life was good.

One day a church member noticed a baby floating down the raging river. The church member quickly ran inside the church to tell the others and ask them to pray for the screaming baby before it went over the fall.

The next day the same church member heard another crying baby floating down the river and then another and another. The church members came out and began praying and evangelizing to the screaming babies as they floated by. Their evangelizing ministry grew as more and more babies floated past. Some members even discussed the need to teach the babies to swim.

One day as they were evangelizing to the drowning babies, one of the church members actually jumped into the water and rescued a baby. The ladies of the church wrapped the half-drowned baby in a small blanket and began caring for the baby. The next day, while church members were in classes learning to improve their evangelizing methods, a couple of church members rescued two more babies. The following day four more crying babies were rescued from the turbulent current. And then eight, then more, and still more! The baby mission began growing so fast they found their church's resources dwindling.

In searching for needed funding, the little church by the river went to other churches in the area for help. One church said there was no sense in helping because they were waiting for the coming of the Lord. Another said that they had disconnected themselves from such worldly issues and were busy building a fortress from the world to worship in. Another church said their rituals and sacraments were most important and time consuming, while another church could not hear the little church because they were preaching their dogma. Another church was too busy making flight arrangements overseas. Then there was the large church whose organizational leaders had little concern outside of growing their church. Another church simply told the little church to call their government representatives because it was their job, not the church's job. Thus, no church wanted to partner with the little church to help rescue the drowning babies.

The little church then went to their local politicians, but they were quickly turned away. Since the babies could not vote, they were not interested.

So, the little church by the river with "hat-in-hand" went to a few wealthy folk and asked them to help. The wealthy investors gave a little to the church. The church gave them praise and gratitude, and the financiers began to feel respected, became enamored by the church's praise and soon became influential members and the biggest proponents of the baby rescue mission.

The little church by the river then heard about and applied for a federal grant. They received a substantial and adequate amount, but were required by the grant to remove their church steeple and remove all their church symbols. The area churches, originally unmoved by the presence of the River Babies, were now horrified by the little church's un-churchy look and blamed the little church for aligning itself with the federal government.

With increased funding, the church quickly organized themselves, setting up watchtowers and training teams of swimmers who could resist the swift waters and rescue more babies. Rescue squads were soon working 24 hours a day. Each day the number of helpless babies floating down the river increased. The church members were efficient, and the rescue squads were now saving many children each day. While not all the babies could be rescued, the church members felt they were doing well to save as many as they could. There were now teams of volunteers who spent all day processing fruit and vegetables for the babies to eat. A dairy farm was dedicated to the purpose of providing milk. The church built baby dormitories where volunteers tended to their needs and sought to place them with loving families.

One day, one of the church members asked, "Where are all these babies coming from? Let's organize a team to go upstream to find out who's throwing all of these babies into the river."

Some church members replied, "The river babies will always be with us." Others said, "Why go upstream, our work is too crucial and over-whelming here downstream." There were those who thought it was too risky to care about upstream matters. Others said, "Don't ask me to get involved, I have nothing left to offer." And others, fearing their funding would stop said, "Our investors who love this rescue mission will be mad." and "This is outside the grant's directives, so we may lose our grant money!"

Isn't this where we find ourselves today? Busying ourselves downstream with no apparent vision to go upstream to rightly stop the flow at its source?

In Louisiana 30 percent of our children under five-years-old are flowing down the raging river of poverty and into Louisiana's increasingly costly prison system. If you or your church is inspired to go upstream, we invite you to join with us at Bridge Ministry of Acadiana. At the Bridge, we do have a river vision of hope for all our children and our churches where the River of Life forever flows down with justice and righteous living for and in all.

But let justice roll on like a river,
righteousness like a never-failing stream!
(Amos 5:24, NIV)

04/06/2010

SENT

As You sent Me into the world, I also have sent them into the world. (John 17:18, NKJV)

How did Bridge decide to move into this neighborhood?

The Bridge story began in 2002 when Trinity Bible Church in Lafayette, La. heard the call to do something within an impoverished neighborhood. Our initial response was with our united prayers asking God: "What urban neighborhood will our church move into? Who in our church will go? How will our church do this? What will our church do in our inner-city? Huh God?"

On February 8-9, 2003, our pastor, Dennis Malcolm, invited his close friend, Jimmy Dorrel, to teach us about Christian Community Development and help us get-up-off-our-good-intentions and get us moving on God's pathway. Jimmy is the originating pastor of the Church Under-the-Bridge in Waco, Texas, pioneered Mission Waco, is a theology professor at Baylor University, and a member and co-founder of the nationally known Christian Community Development Association (CCDA.org).

Jimmy's most profound directive was for us to place an "X" on the map to commit ourselves to a neighborhood, and then move into it. Even though this call to relocate into an impoverished neighborhood was uncomfortable to our safe and secure middle-class minds, we knew down deep that it was the right and faithful way to go. Jimmy also began teaching us the difference between a development mission and a relief mission.

A week after Jimmy visited us on February 16, 2003, about 20 people from Trinity came together to discuss plans. During this first meeting, it was obvious that no one knew what to do, except for one person, Connie Sanders. No one really knew Connie, but she was attuned to hearing God's voice and had been led to visit Trinity only a few months prior to our meeting. We learned that Connie had inner-city, non-profit experience, and a Community Development type degree. Connie quickly became our leader and future Executive Director. It was obvious that God had sent Jimmy and Connie to us for a time such as this.

On April 30, 2003, we began driving and walking around impoverished Lafayette neighborhoods. We also traveled to nine other cities listening and learning from other development inner-city missions about the hands-on theology of *"doing justice, loving mercy, and walking humbly with our Lord"* (Micah: 6:8).

We learned the "Iron Rule" of development was to not do "for" those who can do for themselves, but do things "with" them. Doing "for" can create dependency, while doing "with" develops and empowers people to achieve their dreams for a better tomorrow while respecting their dignity. In talking with our new neighbors, we discovered that relational development is the under-resourced neighborhood's greatest need. We began intently praying for God's blessings of wisdom, vision, strength, and courage.

Soon after leaving the comforts of the four walls of our church, we realized our inner-city mission was too big for one church. So Trinity wisely spun Bridge Ministry of Acadiana out as an independent, non-profit, inter-denominational organization and invited others to join us. *(*The Bridge Ministry of Acadiana received a non-profit 501(c)(3) status on Sept 9, 2003)

Meanwhile, we found a place to rent on Martin Luther King Drive across from the Himbola Apartment complex. The manager told us that it would only take a few days to have this space painted and readied for our occupancy. But, months and months passed and nothing happened. In our prayers we asked God to close the door if this was not the right neighborhood. The door to the Himbola neighborhood never opened for us, but...

Linda Lanclos, a board member, came to a meeting one day with a newspaper article about residents of another nearby neighborhood protesting against drugs, crime, and prostitution. They wanted their streets back. They wanted their children to grow up in a safe neighborhood. As it so happened, Connie had been driving around this neighborhood and stopped at a house a few days earlier. Connie asked a carpenter working on the house if it was for rent. He said, "Yes, and if God is willing, you will rent it." We then asked ourselves, "Why don't we join with this neighborhood?"

On October 1, 2003, we moved into this small house at 308 Huval Street in the middle of a poor, under-resourced neighborhood that, to our surprise, was soon to be known as the "Bridge Neighborhood." At this time, statistics showed that 70 percent of the neighborhood residents had dropped out of high school and 40 percent of Lafayette's drug traffic took place within a one-mile radius from this rent house. Individual income was from $0-$10,000. This was the neighborhood we moved into over nine years ago. But, as proof positive of how "relocation" works in us, our pronouns affectionately and quickly changed from "theirs" to "ours."

On December 3, 2003, we began our asset-based-community-development (ABCD) mapping by walking the streets in the Bridge neighborhood. We were not focusing on the problems so much, but focusing on the assets the neighborhood would begin building upon together. In fear and trembling, we went door-to-door awkwardly introducing ourselves and asking our new neighbors about their life, their dreams, their children, their skills, and their fears.

The first door we knocked on opened slightly with an audible grunt from the woman on the other side. Speaking through a crack in the door, we explained that our mission had moved into the neighborhood a few doors down, and we wanted to talk with her about what she dreamed, thought, and felt. The door flew open, and this wide-eyed lady exclaimed, "No one ever comes into this neighborhood asking us what we think and know!" At this point I knew we were on God's right path.

It was from these "front porch" beginnings that we began humbly taking our first steps toward building relational bridges of love and respect between God, our neighbors, and even ourselves. These porch meetings established the foundation and direction for Bridge's future programing and relationships. Soon our neighborhood residents came together to form their Neighborhood Association, and our neighborhood children began pouring in. Within one year, due to the Bridge's increased numbers, we had to move down the street to a larger house that became available. On God's pathway, God provides.

After moving into the neighborhood, we learned that God had been at work in our neighborhood long before we arrived. We learned that Miss Mary had a large family prayer meeting every week, where her family prayed for the resurrection and redemption of their neighborhood. Miss Mary became our neighborhood Prayer-Warrior, and her son and nephew began leading our neighborhood men's Bible study. Emily, a Bridge Board member who grew up in the house we now rent, mentioned one day that her mother, Miss Nola, had prayed and dreamed for years that her family home would become the neighborhood community center that it is today.

Wow! We excitedly realized that God was in the neighborhood and at work long before we arrived. In humility, any further remnant of any kind of god-complex dissolved.

In 2012, the Lafayette Police Department reported to the Bridge Neighborhood Association that violent crime was down 50 percent and that there had been no murders in 2011. The Neighborhood Association, People Helping People, is winning back their streets. More of our neighborhood children are graduating from high school and going on to higher learning. They are becoming leaders. Our community churches are catching God's vision. Minds and hearts of all ages are being transformed on both sides of the bridge. Crime is going down, and trust is going up.

We thank God our Father, Son, and Holy Spirit for willingly and intentionally moving into our neighborhood here on earth as in heaven. We thank Him for not commuting or living far from us, but humbly moving into our neighborhood with us and in us.

So, how did Bridge decide to move into this neighborhood? We simply followed the Word and Spirit in us. As Christ was sent into our neighborhood, the Bridge was also sent into this neighborhood to reconcile and redeem what has been lost of the Kingdom on earth.

The Word became flesh and blood, and moved into the neighborhood. (John 1:14a, MSG)

12/12/2012

AMACHI

Whatever you did for one of the least of these … you did for Me. (Matthew 25:40b, NIV)

It is the first day of school and the teacher calls role: "Jacodi Jackson." In the back of her classroom a small voice responds, "Here." The teacher immediately looks up and asks, "Is Selena your sister?" The young boy says "Yes." "Ahhh," the teacher says, "she's a tough one. I hope you are not as bad she is."

In his silence, a dim light turns off in the boy's soul. The little boy knows it will be another long year where his teacher will only expect the worst in him. As the teacher's eyes move down to the next name on the role, she wonders, "Why can't I get the good kids, the ones who are competent and care?"

Amachi is an African word, really a question, that means: Who knows what God has brought us through this child?

What if the teacher fully embraced the truth in *amachi*? What if the teacher asked herself: "What has God brought to me through Jacodi today?" Would her mind and heart be more open to God's potential in the mind and heart of little Jacodi? Could *amachi* release her from preconceived expectations and open her mind and heart to dream of what God's great purpose for Jacodi could possibly be?

Embracing *amachi* can not only expand our minds, but will expand our hearts towards Jacodi's, and each child's, wholistic development of both mind and heart. *Amachi* allows us to better see each child's inherent dignity.

The Bridge is not a relief organization, but a development organization that empowers our children to reach their God-given potential, mentally and spiritually. Not teaching down to who they are, but up to who they are to become. Through us, God's long-term caring process develops both minds and hearts and brings out the best in our children.

But, let's also ask, "Who knows what God has brought us through our friends, families, neighborhoods, churches, and institutions? Who knows what God has brought us through our larger community where we love and are loved?"

By expanding our *amachi,* our minds and hearts are opened to the greater possibilities and potential within our larger community that ultimately calls our society up towards greatness too. Thus, *amachi* not only opens our minds and hearts to the latent potential residing in the mind and heart of little Jacodi, but expands our minds and hearts to the latent power within ourselves and our community.

The *amachi* word-question opens us to all possibilities. Herein lies the tremendous human power that is groaning within us to be mobilized, released, and empowered. Together, we actively hope for a better tomorrow, individually and socially. We invite you to come to the Bridge and experience this eye-opening *amachi* hope seen through our active respect and love for everyone. After all, we all are created in the glorious image of God.

God spoke: "Let us make human beings in our image,
make them reflecting our nature...
God created human beings;
he created them godlike, reflecting God's nature."
(Genesis 1:26a, 27a, MSG)

07/25/2011

KIDS SAY THE DARNDEST THINGS!

Connie and the kids were walking in the neighborhood one day, when she overheard one of the boys saying: "When I grow up and go to jail, I'm going to..."

Going to summer camp in the Ozarks, Connie knew the kids would not bring pillows, so she loaded a few pillows from her house for their trip. On the return home all the kids asked: "Can we have these pillows...we ain't got none"

One day I was bringing the kids swimming and one asked me: "Mr. Nelson, when do you get your check?"

Connie and Jennifer were talking with the girls about their fighting, when the girls realized that Connie and Jennifer did not know how to fight. The little girls were shocked, but immediately said: "Ya'll don't know how to fight? You have to know how to fight! We can teach you."

When Linda asked a little boy what he wanted to be when he grew up he said: "I want to be a pimp or a gangster. They make good money."

One of the kids asked me: "Do you smoke?" (I soon learned that he meant crack.)

One very young girl said: "There ain't no good men!"

Once the kids were asked if they knew where the drugs were being sold in the neighborhood. They answered: "Yeah, my uncle," "my mom's boyfriend," "the crack house down the street." They all knew.

A little girl asked: "Where do you live Mr. Nelson?" Before I could answer she quickly followed her question with "Is it safe there?"

"That's my brother's daddy's girlfriend's baby."

One day we learned of a murder in the neighborhood. That afternoon, we had to separate two little girls who were fighting. One yelled to the other, "Why are your people killing my people?"

At our 2004 summer camp, I asked the boys what they wanted to be when they grew-up. Their silent stares shocked me. I soon realized dreaming was a foreign concept.

From their lips, or silent stares, these little children express their realities, fears, and need for safety. Buried deeper inside is their need to be loved and to love. While society wonders why inner-city kids are so hard and fight at school, these kids wonder why society wants them to be so soft and passive. What they are ultimately left to decide as children is whether to be "too soft" for the streets or be "too hard" for the schools. I wonder what I would choose if I were a child and lived in these unsafe Fourth World neighborhoods with low levels of trust and love. Which would you chose?

Yet, in their under-resourced neighborhood there is now a light, a place where these kids have a safe harbor to work, play, develop and be loved. Where "bridge-builders" come from across town to nurture and guide them with daily hands-on-compassion. Trusting and respecting friendships are being built as educational resources and emotional, physical, mental, and spiritual resources flow between us all. And, most important, the children and the neighborhood are beginning to dream dreams of a better tomorrow. Love surely works and is most welcoming to our children.

And whoever welcomes one such child in my name welcomes Me. (Matthew 18:5, NIV)

09/18/2008

THE SIMPLEST OF GIFTS

In viewing the glass as half-empty an organization will become a needs-based organization without any development, boot-straps expectations. Without boot-strap expectations, a needs-based organization will grow and overwhelm an under-resourced neighborhood with need-filling services. But these services may ultimately create more dependency and problems than the neighborhood had before they arrived. The numbers and workload may increase while quality decreases, and the glass is never filled.

When the focus is on a neighborhood's assets, the organization will naturally see the glass as half-full, which leads to development and empowerment. The Bridge Ministry of Acadiana is an asset-based, inner-city mission that has the vision to relationally develop and empower lives educationally, spiritually, and economically—and that being on both sides of the bridge.

Before the Bridge moved into the Four Corners neighborhood, we were taught by inner-city Christian Community Development (CCDA.org) pioneers from Atlanta, Waco, Jackson, and New Orleans that we must first *humbly* walk into these under-resourced neighborhoods to build relationships and to understand their needs.

We were taught to put aside our opinions, and to listen to those in the neighborhood who know their problems better than we do. We were taught that wisdom comes through the door of humility, so we humbly listened. We were also taught to look for the assets within the neighborhood and not so much at the problems. It is from its assets that a neighborhood begins to build and develop, not from its needs.

Our learning process began by going door-to-door asking our neighbors about their dreams for their neighborhood, and what they thought and felt. While on their front porches and usually through cracks in their doors, we would explain that we had moved into the neighborhood to learn and to serve alongside them as friends. Their front doors would then open. One neighbor exclaimed, "No one ever comes into this neighborhood asking what we think!"

With these explosive responses, it was obvious we were on the right path. It was also obvious that this neighborhood in the shadow of Lafayette's downtown had felt neglected and discarded by our community for too long. They felt invisible and ignored in our society, which, outside of murder, may be the worst form of human oppression.

I asked myself: What is it we are giving here that is so important? The answer to my question was that we were simply giving our ears. They finally had someone who was honestly and humbly listening to them and seeing them as part of the solution and not the problem.

As we gave our ears to our neighbors, we began to understand their neglect, their plight, their invisibleness within society, and their struggles in unsafe neighborhoods. By listening and asking questions, we began to understand how government systems, as well as churches and social agencies, many times create more problems than they solve by their one-way impersonal giving. By listening, we began to understand their fears and lack of resources, which can crush the human spirit. By listening, we began to see their dreamless children growing up expecting no more than early death or jail.

We also began to discover the neighborhood's gatekeepers, power-brokers, role-models, and nurturers. We discovered the hidden talents, as well as physical resources like parks and important economic streets. By listening and asking questions, we also learned where God was at work before we arrived. And through listening we began to grow in wisdom and compassion.

By going beyond our "feel-good, better-than-thou" charity, we began to understand and began to respectfully be welcomed as friends. It is in the power of friendship that we now want the best for each other spiritually, educationally, socially, and economically. Yes, we gave our neighbors our ears, but we began by giving our hearts.

During this holiday season our giving alarms will sound off. Yet the best gifts we can give are our simplest gifts. In our under-resourced neighborhood, we have found that by giving our ears, we are now receiving a deeper understanding of God, others, and ourselves, which results in our hearts and minds being enlarged.

So, it is in these greater gifts of love and wisdom that the poor unknowingly give to the rich and is probably why Jesus tells us to *simply love* our neighbors who are not like us... the simplest of gifts maybe to just listen and humbly ask questions.

"After three days they found Him in the temple courts,
sitting among the teachers,
listening to them and asking them questions."
(Luke 2:46, NIV)

12/18/2008

A BOY WAS BORN

A Boy was Born in 1937 without a father. His mother reared him alone until she remarried. His step-father abused him and taught him to steal. The impoverished countryside he grew up in was a violent place where many people carried firearms. This dysfunctional life pattern continued until 1947 when, at the age of ten, he fled to live with his uncle.

His uncle had the most influence on him, second only to the influence of his dysfunctional childhood. His uncle's love of money, love for taking over other people's property, violence, racism, and extremism was unfortunately passed on to the young boy. As the boy grew up, he dropped out of school and became an assassin and brute. At 31, he had earned a fearsome reputation as a political thug, and he became deputy chairman of a renegade political group. This stunted little boy eventually took control of his country and brutally and ruthlessly ruled over it for 22 years. His name was Saddam Hussein.

A Boy was Born into poverty in 1879. His father was an alcoholic, which gradually led to his business failing. He became violently abusive to his wife and child. The boy's mother, a deeply religious woman, was very protective towards him as a child. They uprooted their home at least nine times in his first ten years of life.

His father eventually abandoned his wife and son, cut the family off from all financial support, and left them to fend for themselves.

The town where the boy grew up was a violent, untrusting, and lawless place. It had only a small police force and a culture of violence that included gang-warfare and organized street brawls. He took part in street-fighting as a child, and he was severely beaten on numerous occasions. Permanently scarred from childhood smallpox and having a mildly deformed arm, the boy always felt unfairly treated by life. He developed a strong, romanticized desire for greatness and respect, combined with a shrewd streak of calculating cold-heartedness towards those who had slandered him.

He always felt a sense of inferiority before educated intellectuals and developed a particular distrust toward them. The boy entered seminary school but was expelled, and he later became an atheist. He saw the hypocrisy of the rich, Christian ruling class and their non-care for the poor, the widows, and the fatherless from which his family originated. From his point of view there was no need for the Church, because to him government would better care for the poor.

As he grew into a man, he used his administrative skills and ruthless maneuvering to rid himself of all potential rivals in the Party, first by having many of them condemned and later by ordering them executed. He became the ruthless ruler of his country from 1929-1953. To ensure his position and to push forward, he placed his country on a crash course of collectivization and industrialization. An estimated 25 million farmers were forced onto state farms. Collectivization alone killed as many as 14.5 million people. Later he began ridding the Party of all the people who had brought him to power. It has been estimated that more than 1.2 million party members (more than half the party) were arrested between 1936 and 1939, of which 600,000 died by torture, execution, or perished in the prison. He also purged the military leadership, executing a large percentage of the officer corps. His name was Joseph Stalin.

A Boy was Born in 1889 who was the fourth child of six. His mother was his father's third wife, and also his father's half-niece. He had a troubled childhood, as his father was violent and abusive to him and his mother. As a boy, he was often beaten by his father. A history of family violence committed by his father explains his deep emotional attachment to his mother and deep resentment towards his father. He became an orphan in his teens with very low levels of love in his young life. With no education, he was homeless at times and penniless. Feeling life's injustices were caused by the Jews, he eventually found his meaning in ridding the world of them and trying to create a new world in his image. His name was Adolph Hitler.

NOTE: Billy the Kid, (unknown father); Idi Amin, (abandoned by his father); Khomeini, (father murdered when he was a baby); Ted Bundy, (father unknown); Charles Manson, (unknown father and 16-year-old alcoholic mother); U.S. Prisoners: 95 percent of all male prisoners grew up in homes where fathers were absent, either physically or mentally. Eighty percent of rapists come from fatherless homes. Eighty-five percent of youth in prisons grew up in a fatherless home. Louisiana has the highest fatherless rate in the United States plus the highest incarceration rate in the world.

A boy who is born in a poor, unsafe, untrusting, and dysfunctional inner-city neighborhood, where fighting and dropping-out is the norm, where families are broken and there are no authentic men in the boy's life to admire and guide him, will more often than not go astray. In our safe, middle-class neighborhoods, we ignorantly think it is only a matter for those in generational poverty to pull themselves up by the boot-straps. The problem is if they do, against all odds, pull themselves up by the boot-straps, the boots they put on are many times combat boots, because not trusting and fighting is all they know and have experienced in life.

Mother Teresa wisely said, "The deepest need in a human being is to be loved and to love." What happens inside a person who does not feel loved by healthy and whole families, people, neighborhood, and community?

As we learn from history, they generally gravitate into gangs which meet their deep need to belong and be loved. Here they find a fragile sense of belonging and a contorted sense of significance within their shared anti-social values of hate, prejudice, bitterness, revenge, division, hopelessness, and violence that eventually explodes in the schools, neighborhoods, city, and world. And we wonder why?

But what if? What if a real man enters their young lives (as Jesus entered ours) and admires them, loves them, and guides them? What if their/our neighborhoods, churches, and community nurture them and highly value them? These relationships are a big part of our mission at Bridge Ministry. We believe God loves us all (rich and poor), and God has grand plans for us all that involve community with Him and each other.

> *"For I know the plans I have for you," declares the LORD, "plans to prosper you and not to harm you, plans to give you hope and a future." (Jeremiah 29:11, NIV)*

06/01/2009

THE BLUE TRASHCANS

Our Bridge kids believe President Obama "hung-the-moon." When new, big, blue trashcans with wheels appeared in our Bridge neighborhood after the election this past week, they believed that Mr. Obama had the new trash containers especially delivered to them. They were excited to be so directly touched by the President of the United States.

It's humorous to hear how the children related Mr. Obama becoming our President to the blue trash containers showing up immediately after his taking office. A connection I might have made if viewing the world from their perspective.

Connie, Bridge Executive Director, told them there were also new trucks that were designed to reach out and pick-up each of these specially designed containers and dump trash in the back of the truck. This all could be done with only one driver. Our kids thought this was great.

Connie asked them if they remembered what the old trucks looked like. The kids said they did. Connie then asked them how many men worked on the old trucks. They thought for a minute and said there was one who drove the truck, and two men who hung off the back of the truck "bumping cans." Connie asked the kids what happened to the two men who hung off the back of the truck. The kids didn't know what happened to those two men, so she explained that since the new trucks only needed one man to operate the truck, the two men on the back of the old truck lost their jobs. There were new trucks all over town now.

Through this path of critical thinking the kids were able to see how people's decisions and actions affect people. In these many ways we try to enlighten our children, just as God slowly enlightens us.

"When I was a child, I talked like a child,
I thought like a child, I reasoned like a child.
When I became a man, I put the ways of childhood behind
me. For now we see only a reflection as in a mirror;
then we shall see face to face. Now I know in part;
then I shall know fully, even as I am fully known."
(1 Corinthians 13:11-12, NIV)

06/01/2009

THE RULE OF DETACHMENT

Tiger Wood has the deep desire to win every golf tournament, but this is not his focus. Amid the cameras and buzz, his focus is on addressing the ball immediately in front of him while being totally detached from the "outcome" and his deep desire to win. If he rightly focuses on the ball in front of him, he knows the final score will take care of itself. He has learned that if he focuses on the outcome, he loses his focus on the ball, and he will not be successful. Detaching one's self from the outcome is a hard learned rule for success that requires faith and maturity.

In our non-profit and school circles we hear the terms "measured outcomes" and "test scores." History shows us that a focus on outcomes or test scores is the mind-trap of the immature and a recipe for failure. Yes, we must have a desire for good outcomes, but this should not be our focus. If our focus is on the scoreboard, we will miss the next pitched ball. The correct focus should be on the ball in that moment. As a society, the ball in front of us is creating the fertile, relational soil for people to grow in, and, ironically, detaching ourselves from our desired outcome.

"Still other seed fell on fertile soil. This seed grew and produced a crop that was a hundred times as much as had been planted!"
(Luke 8:8a, NLT—the "seed" in the parable is God's Word)

In the parable from Luke, we see that if seeds are planted in fertile soil, they produce one hundred fold more than was sown. Creating the fertile soil for the seed is most important to focus on, not the harvest.

In relating this parable to our public schools, our focused energy should be toward creating the good and fertile soil around and within every child, and detaching ourselves from their test scores and outcomes. The fertile soil is created through building and maintaining a caring culture of respect. In caringly and truthfully creating this fertile soil of respect, our deep desire for good test scores and outcomes has proven to take care of itself. *

At the Bridge Ministry, we detach from our deep desire for good outcomes and focus on the creation of a caring culture of respect. We understand in faith that our most important focus is on the child in front of us, and not on their future test scores, the buildings, discipline matrix, or media blitzes.

As the world constantly demands outcomes, the Bridge, in faith, focuses on the creation of the fertile soil in and around each child, knowing in faith that our children, families, teachers, and community will be better through our love and respect. This is God's system. Where there is lots of love, there will be lots of learning. This rule of detachment is an act of faith that expresses itself in love.

"The only thing that counts is faith expressing itself through love." (Galatians 5:6, NIV)

* The Jeff Davis Parish School Board's focus is on creating a culture of respect in its school community. As a result, they have the lowest high school dropout rate in Louisiana. As a farming community, they obviously understand the Rule of Detachment and remain focused on creating the good and fertile soil.

07/29/2009

IT WORKS

Jason, our new youth director at the Bridge, asked me to perform a mock-interview with some of our younger Job Club teens. I was so impressed by them that I had a difficult time deciding on who I would hire. As in the real world, I could only hire one.

I asked one young girl what work meant to her. She told me that work was good because God created it, and it is good for one's self-esteem and independence. But, she said she really wants to work so she can help others. Her answer showed a maturity that I found much later in life. I asked another young man if he would work on Saturday. He said he would because he knew many people could not. Another boy gave an impressive response when I asked him what he would do if a grumpy customer came into the store. He smiled and said he would keep a positive attitude in hopes of cheering the person up.

I asked them what they planned to do after graduating from high school. They all wanted to go to college. This is far from the answers I got five and a half years ago when we first entered the neighborhood. At that time no child had a dream for their future. Today they dressed well, sat properly, shook my hand with firmness, and looked me in the eye when they spoke. They have learned to value others, and they are more trusting, trustworthy, and respectful. They all are prepared to take more responsibility and leadership in their own lives and in their community.

I did have one exception to the group, a thirteen year old boy. He forgot and came in with his hat on sideways. He was looking down when he answered my questions. He answered almost all of my questions with "basketball." I asked, "What do you do? What are you good at? What do you do in your spare time? What do you want to do when you graduate from school?" Every answer was "basketball." Ironically, he was the only one who later asked why I did not hire him. I told him why and he said "my bad." He had only arrived at the Bridge six weeks earlier. He was just beginning his exposure to the training we are giving here. As I have experienced the wonderful growth in our children over the years, I know in faith that he will do well, even in basketball.

I left that day awe-inspired and with the full certainty that what God is doing through us at the Bridge works. It is not an overnight success or a quick fix solution, but one that requires a lot of faith and nurturing from day to day over a long period of time. And, *it works.*

He said, "You've been given insight into God's Kingdom – you know how it works" (Luke 8:10a, MSG)

08/04/2009

EXCHANGING PRONOUNS

James Cone wrote a book entitled *The Spirituals and the Blues* where he investigated the thoughts and beliefs of American slaves during their enslavement. Since little was written by the slaves themselves, his question drove him to the study of their songs. It was in their songs he found their deepest expressions of life. So, I wonder what our songs may say about us 150 years from now.

In church last Sunday, I pondered this question. As we sang different songs, I noticed the predominance of the pronouns "I" and "Me" in every song. I began to realize that a sociologist 150 years from now might see our culture through our songs as a very self-focused people with no noticeable value for community. So, in response I began exchanging our songs' pronouns from "I"-"Me" to "Us"-"We" in the latter stanzas of the songs. Something like:

"Jesus loves me this I know, because the Bible tells me so..."
Then exchanging the pronouns later in the song to
"Jesus loves us this we know, because the Bible tells us so..."

While singing, I envisioned the whole congregation singing in harmony the last half of our "Jesus and Me" songs with the newly made-up "Jesus and We" renditions. I began experiencing in my imagination a feeling of *commUnity* in our praise and worship service. I also experienced a sense of loss. I realized how our deep need to be in community with each other, especially within our churches and the larger Body of Christ, is many times thwarted by our over-inflated American cultural value for individualism. It appears that unbridled and unconscious individualism simply knocks the legs out from under community. But herein is the fact: individualism by itself is a lie!

"For none of us lives to himself alone and none of us dies to himself alone" (Romans 14:7, NIV)

The revelation that "Jesus loves Me" is important, foundational, empowering, and motivating. Balancing "Jesus and Me" with "Jesus and We" reflects God's Will for each of us to love both God and other people. Exchanging our pronouns half-way through our songs may be a very small first step in awakening our consciousness to our common-unity.

"A new command I give you: Love one another. As I have loved you, so you must love one another." (John 13:34, NIV)

10/15/2009

FORGIVENESS

"My brothers, as believers in our glorious Lord Jesus Christ, don't show favoritism. [2]Suppose a man comes into your meeting wearing a gold ring and fine clothes, and a poor man in shabby clothes also comes in. [3]If you show special attention to the man wearing fine clothes and say, "Here's a good seat for you," but say to the poor man, "You stand there" or "Sit on the floor by my feet," [4]have you not discriminated among yourselves and become judges with evil thoughts?" (James 2: 1-4, NIV)

One afternoon in a Bible Study with five middle school girls, Connie, our Executive Director, was teaching James 2:1-4. The discussion topic was about excluding someone because of the way they look. This Bible study turned out to be a beautiful healing experience of forgiveness between the young girls present. The girls were asked if they had ever felt excluded by others, and they said "yes." Then Connie asked if they had ever excluded someone else, to which they replied "yes."

This discussion created the space the girls needed to open up about how they felt when they were mistreated by each other based on appearances. The amazing thing that came out of this experience was that the girls were admitting to one another how they had wrongly treated each other and how they desired each other's forgiveness. The more the girls admitted their feelings to one another, the better they felt and the closer they grew together.

One girl said, "This is better than Bible study." Connie replied to her, "This is Bible study in action." They ended the session with a group hug. The remarkable thing is that the girls were asking each other for forgiveness without any authoritative influence. All they needed was the space to be open and honest about how they felt.

Over the years the staff had forced apologies when hurtful words or actions were directed towards another. Rarely were these apologies sincere. At times, fights had erupted as a result. Sometimes even parents would get involved and escalate the fight with one another. We have come a long way, and these girls and all of the kids are learning how to better resolve their differences in caring and right ways that begin with forgiveness.

Much of these things are learned outside of Bible studies when self-controlled adults model forgiveness with each other daily in our children's presence. This helps develop a culture of respect and grace that our children see, feel, and desire. After six years, the children have been growing, and so have we. In all this we give thanks to God for His Divine guidance in all we do at the Bridge Ministry, and we especially thank Him for His forgiveness that sets us all right.

"For I will forgive their wickedness and will remember their sins no more." (Jeremiah 31:34b, NIV)

11/15/2009

AN ADMIRED BOY

"You are my Son, chosen and marked by my love, pride of my life." (Luke 3:22b, MSG)

What God the Father told His Son, Jesus Christ, every boy needs to hear from their father and or an admiring man, "Son, I love and admire you."

Without an admiring father or man in a boy's life, a deep hole develops in a boy's soul that, more often than not, leaves him feeling angry, unworthy, and empty. Our nation's boys are our future men. Many times it takes a lot of faith to envision this future man in the boy in front of us.

For this vision, it takes not only an admiring older man, but a faithful one too. It takes a man that can, in faith, see past the boy toward the authentic man they are designed to become. It takes a faithful and admiring man who is able to believe in the young boy for a long enough time for the boy to finally believe in himself.

I'll call him Tom in this story. Tom, at age 16, moved into the Bridge neighborhood. As a fatherless high school dropout, he was allowed to do nothing and had no dreams of where he was going. He had no man in his life that admired him enough to call him up. He is now 18 years old.

It was at Bridge that Duane met and began to encourage Tom to work toward his GED (high school equivalency test). Duane and Tom now work together most days building gates and doors at a friend's horse farm and doing classroom work together. As trust between Duane and Tom grows, Tom is becoming more open to Duane. As Tom opens up, Duane is better able to assess the specific resources Tom needs and how to best help him in his struggles.

A few weeks ago, Duane told me in front of Tom that "Tom knows much more than he realizes. He's very smart." Upon hearing this praise, I felt Tom's chest swell within his 6'2" frame, and he gave an admiring glance towards Duane. Their mutual admiration has now become a two-way bridge where edifying resources can best flow in both directions.

Duane now understands Tom's past school issues were related to math because Duane saw Tom's frustration in doing the simple measurements needed in carpentry. He told Tom they would begin working with the basic multiplication flash cards first. Tom held out his hand and said, "Thank you Mr. Duane."

Working to repair the sink at the Bridge the other day, Tom said, "Mr. Duane, let me crawl under the sink, I can do it." And he did do it, as Duane watched alongside. Tom with his great smile later told Duane, "This was a good day, thanks."

There are many things that constantly pull an under-resourced boy down. Among them is peer pressure. It is common in under-resourced neighborhoods for a boy's peers to laugh at him in the group when he messes up.

In their fear of being laughed at by the group, a young boy will often freeze-up and stop trying in his effort to appear cool and not look stupid. Duane now wants to create more one-on-one time, having realized that when Tom is separated from his peers, he is much more open to trying, learning, and growing. In this one-on-one time, the inner emotional cushion needed for our future men to ultimately stand-up against their peers and the world's arrows is created.

The boys in the Bridge neighborhood like to have fun, often at the expense of each other. This is their humor, but sometimes it can drag them down instead of lifting them up. In time they, as a group, may begin to believe they are as worthless as they tell each other and the world tells them they are. They all need a faithful and admiring man to stand beside them and tell them, "This is not so. You are much more than your streets or the world says you are. I see the greatness God has created in you. You are created in the image of God, and I want you to experience all that God has uniquely created you to be. You have what it takes, and I love you and admire you and believe in you. You can do it. As God has promised to be with us, I'll be with you for the long haul."

Simply put, admiring and respecting the human dignity of others is what we do at the Bridge—especially for our fatherless and rarely admired children.

"God created man in His own image;
in the image of God He created him" (Genesis 1:27a, NKJV)

02/01/2010

CHURCH DECLINE AND ASCENT

"A new command I give you: Love one another.
As I have loved you, so you must love one another.
By this everyone will know that you are my disciples,
if you love one another."
(John 13:34-35, NIV)

In *Bowling Alone*, Robert Putnum graphically illustrates how Americans, as a percentage of the population, are attending churches less and less since the mid-sixties. With attendance declining in our churches, there is an accompanying loss of its influence in the social, political, and economic life of America and abroad. To Putnam, Christian social capital is at its lowest level.

From another perspective, Albert Mohler of the Southern Baptist Theological Seminary reports in *Newsweek* about the decline in the number of Americans who call themselves Christian (www.newsweek.com/id/192583).

CNN reports "America is a less Christian nation than it was 20 years ago, and Christianity is not losing out to other religions, but primarily to a rejection of religion altogether." (www.cnn.com/2009/LIVING/wayoflife/03/09/us.religion.less.christian)

Why is the Church declining, and what does an attractive church look like?

Let us examine the primitive church in the Book of Acts for an understanding of how the original Church grew so contagiously. First, the primitive church was not selfish or materialistic. They lived by sharing and committing their lives to each other in community. This started with the ethnocentrists, those who believed in the superiority of their own ethnic race.

"Many were added" to the ancient Church, but only after they had broken down their feelings of superiority and began to build relational bridges to those who were not like themselves. Church history shows that the church grew in unity and numbers as they continually built bridges of friendship across social, cultural, ethnic, economic, and racial divides.

"..many who heard the message believed, and the number of men grew to about five thousand." (Acts 4:4, NIV)

The first bridge built by the Acts Church was between the Hebrew Christian Jews and the second class Greek Christian Jews. It began when the Greek Jews complained that their widows were being discriminated against in their food allotment by the Hebrew Jews. To settle this issue, the Hebrew Christian Jews placed seven well-respected and holy men in charge of the provisions. The men placed in charge were all Greek, and, the bridge of reconciliation between the Hebrew and Greek Jews was respectfully built. It was reported: "The numbers of believers greatly increased in Jerusalem and many Jewish priests were converted too." (Acts 6:7, NLT)

The second bridge built in the Acts Church was

between the Christian Jews and the half-breed and hated Samaritans. It began with the martyrdom of Stephen at the feet of Saul, (Acts 7:59) which was followed by much persecution (Acts 8:1). Due to the persecution, many Jewish and Hebrew Christians fled to Judea and Samaria. It was to the town of Samaria that Phillip, a Greek Christian, went for refuge and then continued telling others about the Messiah. Samarian crowds listened intently and saw many miracles, believed, and received much joy (Acts 8:6-8). Back in Jerusalem, the apostles heard that the hated Samarians were accepting God's message, so they sent Peter and John to see if this was even possible. After seeing the transformation in the Samaritans, Peter and John continued "testifying and preaching the word of the Lord in Samaria," (Acts 8:25, NLT) and on returning to Jerusalem, they stopped in many more Samarian villages along the way.

The third bridge was built by Philip to a black man from Ethiopia, Africa. Seeing the Ethiopian, he sat with him and explained scripture to him. The man believed and was baptized, and then Phillip continued on his way. Meanwhile, in the Greek communities of Lydda and Joppa (twenty-five miles west of Jerusalem), the barriers between the Hebrew and the Greek Jews continued to dissolve and "many believed in the Lord." (Acts 9:42, NIV)

The fourth bridge built in the Acts Church was between the Christian Jews and the lowly and unclean Gentiles. The vision for this bridge came in a dream to Peter. Peter later states, after being called by Cornelius, a Gentile, "I now realize how true it is that God does not show favoritism but accepts men from every nation who fear him and do what is right." (Acts 10:34-35,

NIV) Cornelius and his family were then received and baptized. At this time, some of the believers who had fled persecution were also reaching out to the Gentiles in Antioch building relational bridges of friendship to them. And, "a great number of people believed." (Acts 11:21, NIV)

It was in Antioch that believers were first called Christians (Acts 11:26). It was here that the mostly Gentile "daughter church" in Antioch graciously donated famine relief to their mostly Jewish "mother church" in Jerusalem. And the churches were committed to each other in their unity and brotherly love.

Due to the social, ethnic, economic, and racial barriers being boldly broken down, the Antioch Church was now known by its diversity and international make-up. In Acts 13:1, the leaders were described as Simeon, a black man; Lucius from Cyrene, northern Africa; Manaen, a childhood companion of King Herod of Antipas; and Saul, a rabbinic Jew and Roman citizen. It was this authentic church community in their city that then became the missional church, as they "placed their hands on them (Paul and Barnabas) and sent them off." *(*Acts 13:3, NIV)

Paul and Barnabas were called to live and love elsewhere, as the larger church community answered their call to live, love, and thrive in their city of Antioch. Thus, the first incarnational mission began, and many more Gentiles were ultimately infected with the irresistible influence of God's love.

When people courageously go beyond their social, ethnic, economic, and racial prejudices and reach out the hand of friendship to others not like themselves, they will grow individually and collectively. When people go beyond their self-centeredness, materialism, and ethnocentrisms and give of themselves, they will grow. When the Jewish Christian Church built those historic bridges of brotherly love to the Greek Jews, and their neighbors, the Samaritans and the Gentiles, they became better and healthier and irresistibly attractive and inclusive. They grew.

But, the Antioch Church grew not only by breaking down the age old barriers, but also due to its relational actions of love to the oppressed and wounded. The Church was always thinking of others and not itself. They were the living proof of a loving God to a hurting, burdened and confused world.

The Early Church "drawing men out of their social environments into an organization expressively dedicated to the achievement of this high moral standard is a wonderful testimony to the society-making power of the new religion. Jews were wrenched loose from the firm hold of their race and religion; Greeks were wrenched from their culture and pleasures; and both joined together on a footing of equality. Spiritual affinity triumphed over the strongest natural bonds that hold men together... the force of which can only be measured by the obstacles it had to overcome." (*Christianity and the Social Crisis* by Walter Rauschenbusch; page 118)

God's trumpet calls for His Body to connect in unity within God's revealed Will to love ourselves, as well as others. God's trumpet calls out for His Body to intentionally and courageously build relational bridges out from our own little individual silos and stories to others not like ourselves. Then the Church Body will become attractive and relevant again in our American cities and beyond, living out noble stories within God's larger epic story of reconciliation and redemption.

"All the believers were one in heart and mind."
(Acts 4:32a, NIV)

02/03/2010

ECONOMICS 101

"I will instruct you and teach you in the way you should go; I will counsel you with my loving eye on you." (Psalm 32:8, NIV)

In one of Duane Swanson's recent economic classes at Bridge, he and two of our teens dug an eighty-foot trench in order to lay a PVC line for a single mom who was able to only pay a modest amount for the work. Before they began working, they prepared a business proposal to present to the client. This included calculating the length of the trench, the cost of renting the trencher, buying other necessary supplies, and the time involved to get the job done. The woman accepted their proposal, and the work began.

Duane then asked the boys if they wanted to make another $100? Well, they sure did. Duane explained they had the option to dig the trench or rent a trenching machine for a hundred dollars. He explained that if they decided to dig the trench themselves, they could both share the hundred dollars saved from not renting the trencher. They eagerly decided to dig instead of renting.

At the end of the first day, one of the exhausted teens complained that his arms, his legs, his back, and even his toes were sore! He said he did not want to do this for a living and vowed that he was now going to college or technical school.

And so it goes, digging trenches in ninety-eight degree weather has been found by many great men to be the best economics class and motivator they ever experienced. A lot of good men with shovels in their hands make those deep vows in these trenches. Such vows were already being uttered by one of these future men in their first of four days in the trenches of Bridge Economics 101.

It is so important for our under-resourced inner-city boys and girls, to have a good mentor teaching them in the trenches of their lives. These relational rewards will benefit them throughout their lives with their community, family, and work. Duane walks his talk and works alongside these young people even in the hottest of days. He recently took early retirement from Chevron to donate more time at Bridge Ministry of Acadiana. This past semester, he began the "Jobs For Life" program with the neighborhood's high-schoolers and drop-outs. The successes in his life as an engineer and father have empowered him to better enter his second half of life with significance. He is another quiet hero that I am honored to call my friend, as are our young boys.

Our ultimate hope is for our children to become whole, capable, and caring family members and citizens.

UPDATE:

During time with Duane, one young boy caught a vision for his life as an electrician. In 2013, he graduated from our local community college with Residential and Commercial Electrical Degrees. While the boy is on the path to success, Duane continues on his path to significance through breathing life into others.

Thank you, Lord, for your great plans for us all. This boy's story would not be the same without mentioning that after this summer job with Duane, this fatherless 16-year-old boy lost his mother. With much daily love and encouragement in his life at Bridge, he found the strength and endurance to persevere on a path towards achieving his vision for a better tomorrow with God and others. Our hopes are that he too will move from a life vision of success to one of significance.

"For I know the plans I have for you," declares the Lord, "plans to prosper you and not to harm you, plans to give you hope and a future."
(Jeremiah 29:11, NIV)

02/03/2010

HIGHER EXPECTATIONS

"Whoever welcomes this little child in my name welcomes me...." (Luke 9:48a, NIV)

One of my friends is a Communicative Disorders Professor at the University of Louisiana Lafayette. He explained to me that their research pertaining to overcoming stuttering has proven that it is not a therapist's diplomas, technique, experience, money, equipment, or programs that are the key to their client's success. The key to success is the therapist's high expectations for their client.

What we expect, all too often, is exactly what we get. Nowhere is this truer than in education, where teachers' expectations of students are crucial. Whether or not a teacher is aware of it, self-fulfilling prophecies can impact students either to the child's benefit or detriment. (http://info.greenwood.com/books/0275955/0275955028.html)

Self-fulfilling prophecy is a concept developed by Robert K. Merton to explain how an expectation, whether correct or not, affects the outcome of a situation or the way a person (or group) will behave. For example, labeling someone a criminal, and treating that person as such, may foster criminal behavior in the person subjected to this expectation. (http://encyclopedia.com/articles/11668.html)

The concept of the self-fulfilling prophecy can be summarized in four key principles: 1) We naturally form certain expectations of people or events. 2) We communicate those expectations with various cues. 3) People tend to respond to these cues by adjusting their behavior to match them. 4) The result is that the original expectation becomes true.

This creates a circle of self-fulfilling prophecies. (http://westrek.hypermart.net/mngmnt_artcls/motivate_02b.htm)

Let's flesh this out. If you are a teacher and a teen comes into your classroom with piercings and tattoos, what are your expectations? What are your expectations of a child who comes into your classroom whose rebellious brother and sister you taught in previous years? What would be your expectations of an Asian student whose parents you know both teach math at the local university? According to your expectations, which student do you want to teach or not?

Sometimes we are quick to decide if a child is worthy or not. Many times the child deemed unworthy by a teacher is also deemed unworthy by society. Everyone is telling that child they are unworthy, and the child begins to believe it. They begin to negatively act on what is projected toward them and unknowingly live out these self-fulfilling prophecies of who their neighborhoods and society tell them they are.

Yet, when a faithful, caring, and capable adult takes enough time to break through the child's tough protective armor, they often find a frightened, hurt, abused, and/or lonely child who hungers for love and security. After breaking, fertilizing, and watering the hard soil of the child's soul, the once hard to love child is now hard not to love as their roots of trust reach deeper in our souls and the dark thistles and vines of our low expectations are removed. Yet, the garden still needs to be faithfully maintained and weeded so the child gets adequate nourishment and sunlight to grow straight and tall and ultimately agree with God's great plans and vision for them.

At the Bridge, we lovingly believe all children deserve equal access to high expectations and bright futures. Equal access to bright futures means equal access to different relationally transferred resources: education resources, positive role models, spiritual resources of love and respect, safety and security resources, social and workplace etiquette resources, self-control resources, God's Word and promises, etc. But it takes more than just access; it takes a child's willingness to acquire these needed resources too. This willingness is birthed in their trust in the adult who encourages, respects, and loves them daily in their long term struggle to mature and become whole.

So, how can we rise above the trappings of our own low expectations? To vault us above our expectations we must first stand on the fact that all people are created in the image and likeness of God (Genesis 1:26-27), and their human dignity and sacredness deserves respect. In this we at the Bridge ask "What are God's great expectations for this child in front of me?" This question opens our consciousness to all of God's possibilities. This higher consciousness is based in love, which *never fails*!

"If you love someone, you will be loyal to him no matter what the cost. You will always believe in him, always expect the best of him, and always stand your ground in defending him. All the special gifts and powers from God will someday come to an end, but love goes on forever."
(1 Cor 13:7-8, TLB)

03/09/2010

TAKE IT WITH A SMILE!

"Children, do what your parents tell you. This is only right. Honor your father and mother is the first commandment that has a promise attached to it, namely, so you will live well and have a long life.
(Ephesians 6:1-3, MSG)

I grew up in Monroe, LA, and I excelled in most sports, but pole vaulting was my true love. I was proud of my accomplishments and attached my identity to my physical abilities. In my first few weeks of college, this identity was suddenly shattered. It happened in a high-speed drunken car accident that left one of my best friends dead. I was paralyzed from the neck down.

My parents flew in to be with me in what must have felt like the longest flight of their lives. During my mom's first few hours in the hospital room, the shock of my spinal injury hit her as she placed a mirror in my lifeless hands, and it fell on my chest. She immediately said, "Nelson, you have no other choice but go to college, as you will never be able to do physical labor." This may sound a bit harsh, but the truth was exactly what I needed to hear. Mom lovingly stayed in the room with me for the next two months feeding me, bathing me, scratching my nose, etc. Dad had to go back to work, but called daily. I slowly regained about 80 percent movement, but I had to wear a full body brace for the next year. I was eighteen years old. It was 1967.

I only tell this story to illustrate my mother's remarkably strong and resilient attitude in the midst of the pain any mother would feel for a child with such a critical injury. She never tried to fix-it or to excuse me from my physical struggle. She embraced it as if it was her own. She and my dad encouraged me every step of the way. They never allowed me to drift into self-pity or abdication from life. With that immediate comment to me in the hospital that day, she cast a new vision for me, one that spoke in love and truth to me. Self-pity was simply not an option. And, to her, there was no other option but college if I ever hoped to find a meaningful and purposeful vocation and become economically self-sufficient. I wonder what life would have been like without this tough-love vision she cast that day.

Forty-three years later, my mom is eighty-eight years old and living alone in Monroe surrounded by many caring friends and a wonderful neighborhood. Her church also embraces her and watches out for her, as my brother and I live a few hundred miles away. Saying she is not in good physical condition is an understatement. It is a painful struggle for her just to move about, and falling is an ever-present possibility. However, her love of God and people motivates and drives her on. She is still cooking three full meals a day, and she dresses and puts on lipstick as she greets her daily flow of friends and answers her many phone calls. Remarkably, in spite of pain, she is always ready to go and has a smile on her face. Her motto on a hand written refrigerator-note is "*Take It With A Smile!*"

Thanks, Mom, for your wisdom to allow me to struggle and learn to *"Take It With A Smile."* I know it was not easy to enter into and watch my pain. Thanks, Mom, for living the vision of how to grow old gracefully. Happy Mother's Day, Mom. You are truly a blessing.

NOTE:

This was written 5/5/2010. My Mom, Virginia Ann Nelson Warner, moved to Heaven on 6/1/2013. She was 91 years old. Her final dream was fulfilled in being able to leave her home "feet-first." Now her refrigerator note is framed and hanging on my office wall. See you and dad soon...☺

05/05/2010

IT DOESN'T FEEL GOOD

"Stop judging by mere appearances, but instead judge correctly." (John 7:24, NIV)

I was excited that afternoon six years ago as I was driving to the swimming pool to swim a few laps. This was the first day of my latest exercise plan. Failed ones in the past loomed in my mind. I was in hope that this latest undertaking would not be added to the list of past failures.

After changing into my swim trunks, I jumped into the pool and got started. After only a few laps, I had to stop and catch my breath. While I gasped for air, I noticed a young boy paddle up to me. He looked to be about ten. I just smiled and started another lap. As I came to the end of the lap, the boy was there again. I realized that he was pulling himself along the rope on the lane just behind me.

As I would finish a lap and turn, he would let go of the rope and act like he was swimming. I told him he was doing great. We "swam" another lap together and, as I expected, he was there again paddling up behind me. I told him he may become a great swimmer by starting at such an early age. I said he had what it takes, and he beamed in response to my admiration and encouragement.

On the next lap we found his older sister standing above us glaring down, "Jamie get out of the pool right now!" He did not move, and that irritated her all the more. I told him that he should follow her. He said, "She's always bossing me around." After she stormed off, I turned and we swam another lap together.

On our return, Jamie's mother and sister were both standing there above us with their hands on their hips. His mother glared down at him while totally ignoring me, and commanded him to leave the pool "pronto*!*" I felt his sister staring at me in disgust while his mother stood waiting for him to get moving. I could see Jamie's defeated frame sag as he climbed out of the pool, and I could sense turmoil in his little soul.

Also, I felt a disturbance brewing within me. Then, Jamie's mother shifted her focus onto me. She looked down on me in the pool with penetrating eyes that spoke of her judgment of me. Yet, nothing was said as she quickly turned and walked away with Jamie and his sister in tow. In shame, Jamie did not look my way.

As they were leaving, his sister looked at me with a cold stare as if she knew all about me. For the first time in my life I realized that I was the victim of prejudice. They did not even know me, and yet they instantly judged me as a sexual-predator. Of that, I have no doubt. I felt extremely violated, even though their judgment was leveled without a word being said. It did not feel good.

In mulling over all this, I began to get angry and could still feel the pain of this well-aimed dagger deep in my chest. As I got into my car to leave, I noticed a black man walking closely past my car. I automatically locked my doors. The black man heard the doors lock, and he knew without a word being spoken of my judgment of him. Now I know that *It Doesn't Feel Good.*

"Do to others as you would have them do to you."
(Luke 6:31, NIV)

06/14/2010

THANKING ALL FATHERS

"As men go, so goes society, so goes the community,
So goes the church, and so goes the family."
(Men's Fraternity Philosophy)

In the Pilanesberg National Park in northwestern South Africa, Rangers have reported that young bull elephants have become increasingly violent, especially to white rhinos. Apparently, the aggressiveness is a byproduct of government programs to reduce elephant populations by killing the bigger older male animals.

Almost all of the young rogues were orphaned when they were calves, depriving them of adult male contact. Under normal circumstances, the dominant older males keep the young bulls in line and serve as role models for them. In the absence of that adult influence, juvenile delinquents grow up to terrorize their neighbors. The absence of adult role models, early supervision and discipline is often catastrophic— for elephants, as well as for teenagers.

The Problem Identified-The Solution Found

"...The killings clearly weren't the work of poachers. The rhinos' horns hadn't been touched. The park rangers began conducting an investigation. Their first findings led them to believe that if they were to round up the usual suspects, they'd need a pretty large holding pen."

That's because the prime suspects were not humans, but elephants. It turned out that young male elephants were behind the murders of Pilanesberg's rhinos. Why would they do it? Well, like most juvenile delinquents, they had grown up without role models.

"I think everyone needs a role model, and these elephants that left the herd had no role models and no idea of what appropriate elephant behavior was," said Gus van Dyk, Pilanesberg Park's field ecologist.

The problem goes back 20 years to South Africa's largest conservation area, Kruger National Park. Kruger had too many elephants. In those days there was no way to relocate these large adults. So researchers decided to kill the adults and save the young elephants, which were more easily transported to other parks.

The government veterinarian who originally approved the relocations, Dr. Hym Ebedes, said it was a good idea. He said that he considered the possibility that the young elephants might not adjust well, but that there was no history and no other option. The intentions may have been good, but the program created a whole generation of traumatized orphans thrown together without any adults to teach them how to behave.

Years later, those lonely orphans developed into troubled teenagers. That's when the rhino killings at Pilanesberg Park began. Like a police department facing a crime wave, the rangers photographed the murder scenes and put together rap sheets on the prime suspects, giving them each names.

In addition to killing rhinos, the young rogues

acted aggressively toward tourist vehicles. Researchers eventually decided to kill five of the young male elephants. They may have been just juvenile delinquents, but there's no reform school for elephants.

McMillan, who cares for the elephants at a private reserve near the park, began studying the herd. At that point, there was still time to study the situation, because a real confrontation was several years away. The elephants on his reserve were still too small to attack a rhino.

McMillan followed the elephants constantly to document the rhino attacks. At first the scenes seemed funny enough: One day, Mafuta hosed down a rhino with his trunk. But the attacks became more violent. At one point Mafuta spent seven hours stubbornly going after a group of rhinos. When McMillan briefly managed to distract the elephant, the rhinos ran for cover. But when Mafuta saw what had happened, he charged off in a rage. Several weeks later he attacked one of the same rhinos again.

"This time he actually got on top of her and pushed her down, knelt on her, went around the back and kicked her," McMillan said. After another attack, he decided to shoot Mafuta.

"I wasn't happy," said McMillan. "I realized it had to be done, but because I had been working rather closely with the animal, you form emotional attachments."

The people at Pilanesberg also wanted to avoid killing the delinquents. As they studied the elephants, a pattern began to emerge. The elephants picking on the rhinos were suffering from an excess of testosterone. The solution turned out to be the biggest Big Brother program in the world.

The rangers began looking for role models to keep the youngsters from mating at an early age when they couldn't handle those raging hormones. They decided to bring in some even larger adult male (bull) elephants. In 1998, the rangers at Kruger National Park brought in some of these big male elephants in specially designed trucks. No one had ever tried to move elephants that large before.

The bigger, older elephants established a new hierarchy, in part by sparring with the younger elephants to discourage them from being sexually active. That means less testosterone, and that's good news for the rhinos. Van Dyk compared it to a group of teenagers who have been acting up and are all of a sudden confronted by their fathers.

The Pilanesberg juveniles seem to be reading the message loud and clear. Since the big bulls arrived, not one rhino has been killed.

- http://www.cbsnews.com/stories/2000/08/22/60II/main226894.shtml?CMP=ILC-SearchStories (7/18/2001).
- Also, it appears that the original story came from: http://www.time.com/time/magazine/article/0,9171,987172-1,00.html
- Also "Bringing Up Boys" by James Dobson (copyright 2001)

Interestingly, God tells us through the prophet Isaiah that the same that happened with the elephants will happen in our neighborhoods and society when real men are removed:

He's withdrawing police and protection, judges and courts, pastors and teachers, captains and generals, doctors and nurses, and, yes, even the repairmen and jacks-of-all-trades. He says, "I'll put little kids in charge of the city. Schoolboys and schoolgirls will order everyone around. People will be at each other's throats, stabbing one another in the back: Neighbor against neighbor, young against old, the no-account against the well-respected. One brother will grab another and say, 'You look like you've got a head on your shoulders. Do something! Get us out of this mess.' And he'll say, 'Me? Not me! I don't have a clue. Don't put me in charge of anything.'" (Isaiah 3:2-7, MSG)

At Bridge Ministry, we do have a clue and a hope of a better tomorrow for our fatherless neighborhood. As to Fathers, our world would be much different without you. THANKS MEN!

06/15/2010

THE POWER OF FRIENDSHIP

"If whatever we do does not end in love, we are simply wasting our time." (Rev Charles Hill)

Claude has been living in the Bridge neighborhood his whole life. His father was a retired police officer. Growing up in the neighborhood he has seen and heard many things over the years and knows all too well how the streets consistently deal out misery to the young and old alike. With his untrusting and well-founded mindset, Claude does not allow his two beloved children to leave their yard.

Over two years ago, he heard that some Christian organizations, Rebuilding Together, Trinity Bible Church and Bridge Ministry of Acadaina joined together to rebuild a hurricane damaged house for a single-parent family in the neighborhood. Claude's wall of mistrust began to slowly crumble as he watched as volunteers came into the neighborhood and real friendships were being made. Claude began to learn more about the Bridge and then made the big move to entrust his son to our care at the Bridge. Then two years ago, Claude had to have surgery.

Meanwhile, Bridge staff members Jason and Lacey,

were called to move into the Bridge neighborhood where they began making new friends with the neighbors they were humbly and respectfully called to live alongside. They originally drove one hour each way to work at the Bridge, until they finally found a home to purchase in the neighborhood, which was near Claude's home. Now, Jason and Lacey walk together to work every day.

Recently Jason was talking with Claude, as neighbors do, and learned that Claude had to go back into the hospital due to a post-surgery complication. Jason offered to mow Claude's yard while he was recuperating. Claude suspiciously asked "how much?" Jason replied, "Neighbors don't charge neighbors for such things". The man gave Jason a wary look.

Claude went back into the hospital, and Jason mowed his yard during his recuperation. Now, when Claude is mowing his yard and sees that Jason's yard needs mowing, Claude crosses the street to mow Jason's yard too. Next week Jason is going to California. While he is gone, Claude and his wife have promised to look in on Jason's wife, Lacey; and, as neighbors do, Claude will be mowing Jason's yard. Doing as Neighbors do, illustrates how our streets are won back through trusting and friendly neighbors who do what neighbors do, and know what is going on around them.

Jason's neighborly act of mowing Claude's yard planted a seed. This may never have happened if Jason did not respectfully live in the neighborhood and take the initiative to get to know Claude better as a friend and neighbor. It is in the power of friendships that our neighborhood streets are won back from drugs and prostitution and our old barriers of mistrust are broken down. Our encounters and how we faithfully interact in them, are huge in God's eyes as bridges of friendships and community are rebuilt anew. It is in these safe environments that all our children thrive and grow, and our elderly can safely sit on their porches and in their parks again, while children respectfully play around them. Ironically, in seeking the peace and prosperity in our neighborhood, we are finding our own prosperity.

"Also, seek the peace and prosperity of the city to which I have carried you into exile. Pray to the LORD for it, because if it prospers, you too will prosper."" (Jeremiah 29:7, NIV)

08/07/2010

NEW CARING, NEW THINKING, NEW BEHAVIOR

Love the Lord your God with all your heart and with all your soul and with all your mind and with all your strength. (Mark 12:30, NIV)

Our schools and churches have by and large utilized the "teach-me" and "feed-me" consumer-type learning environment (classroom setting, self-help talks, sermons, Bible studies, conferences, lectures, etc.). Our learning is based on the Greco-Roman model of learning, which focuses on transferring ideas and concepts.

The Greco-Roman paradigm believes a human can think their way into a new way of acting. In this paradigm, information is of the highest value, while action and reflection is of lower value. For hundreds of years our learning institutions have been built on this academic model. It's a model that rates books and intellect higher than practical experiences, and even caring, requiring much "head" with little "heart" and "hand" involvement.

This learning model alone is not the best way to learn. When I graduated from college and excitedly got a job as a geologist with a major oil company, the older professional geologists in the Lafayette Geologic Society said, "Nelson, you are now entering the real world where you will have to make A's every day." They were telling me that my learning as a real geologist was just beginning. For me, the Greco-Roman model of learning had finally come to an end.

On the other hand, the Hebrew model that Jesus used to teach his disciples, was life-on-life focused that was relational, real, and relevant. The Hebrew model was not concerned solely with ideas and concepts like the Greek method, but also with the implementation of these ideas and concepts. Jesus knew that His disciples would not be transformed by the transfer of information lived apart from practical applications.

Jesus knew that the transformation and development of our hearts, minds, and actions cannot happen outside of our active and loving relationships with God, self, and neighbors. It was Jesus, who in intimate relationships with His disciples, modeled this holistic development truth that he wished to convey. "Follow me," he repeatedly said.

Jesus knew we need to be taught to think our way into a new way of acting, and also be taught to act our way into a new way of thinking. Jesus Christ takes aim at our hearts from our minds, from our bodies, and from our souls. As to man's character development, Jesus knew that the heart of the matter was a matter of our hearts.

This holistically engaging Hebraic model was Jesus's method of making wise disciples who later became the leaders of the world's greatest movement. His loving, physical, and spiritual actions produced mature disciples that were empowered to teach. As Jesus' disciples were being more fully equipped by the indwelling Spirit and His word, Jesus said, *"Therefore go and make disciples" (Matt 28:19a, NIV)*

10/05/2010

FLYING LESSON

"I'm not here to fix your struggle,
I'm here to embrace your struggle." (John M. Perkins)

While hunting in South Texas one November morning, I shot a quail that fell into an overgrown ravine. My bird dogs immediately ran into the overgrowth to "hunt dead." As I reached the bottom of the gulley, I found myself in another world. Inside a tunnel in the gulley's overgrowth, there were a million butterflies resting. They were part of the annual butterfly migration through South Texas.

During this migrations time, it is possible to see mile-long stretches of butterflies flying south and into Mexico. Yes, butterflies migrate thousands of miles, but as remarkable as this is, it is not the most remarkable part of their journey.

The most remarkable part of their journey begins when a caterpillar builds its cocoon. About a month later a beautiful new creation struggles to break free of the cocoon and fly. If a caring person wanted to help the butterfly in its struggle by opening the cocoon, the butterfly would never be able to fly. For it is in this struggle out of the cocoon that it develops the necessary muscles to fly. Sometimes with our best intentions, we can cause great harm to young, weak butterflies… and to our children.

It appears very unloving to allow an animal or a person to remain in their struggle when we can help, and it appears very compassionate and heroic to relieve an animal or person from the burden of their struggle. Yet from the above example this is often not true. If we are to become truly merciful, our understanding of the true nature of the struggle is paramount and should dictate how our charity should rightly and justly respond.

Generally, there two types of charity: relief charity and development charity. In relief charity, we say “Yes, I will relieve you from your struggle, because you are bleeding to death.” We are motivated by our hearts and do the work through our hearts and feelings. If relief is rightly done, it should be a relatively short-term effort. After relief (mercy) rightly ends, development (tough-love) begins.

In development charity, one has to learn to say no to our immediate tendency to relieve another person from their struggle. In development (after the bleeding has stopped) we must learn to say “No, I cannot do for you what you can do for yourself, but I will be with and alongside you.” In development we are motivated by our hearts (love), but must work from our heads. Development is a long-term relational mission. Historically in America our greater need is in development, yet the vast majority of our resources goes towards relief; and, we wonder why people become bitter, and not better.

At Bridge Ministry, we are a development or empowerment mission, not a relief mission. We do not envision our children as caterpillars, but as the butterflies they are to become. In our long term and faithful effort, we do not attempt to relieve our children of their daily struggles, but lovingly embrace their struggle and walk alongside them encouraging them to become all that God has designed them to become. By doing "with," not 'for," people are empowered. They learned and accomplished a task, and they are enabled to become economically self-sufficient.

What is true for our children's economic struggles, is also true for our spiritual struggles. We cannot be transformed spiritually while remaining within the comfortable cocoons of our church. After we struggle from of our cocoons and go love our neighbors, our hearts and minds are transformed into a new and deeper consciousness for community, faith, and love that bring meaning and purpose to us all. So struggling out of our spiritual cocoon is part of our journey of transformation too. We are empowered to fly higher when we cross the bridge to meet our neighbors, embrace each other's struggles, and become friends.

"Everyone sees it. God's work is the talk of the town.
Be glad, good people! Fly to God!"(Psalms 64:9, MSG)

11/12/2010

GOD'S PATHWAY

"Follow Me", Jesus said (Matthew 4:19, NIV)

Seven years ago, when we began Bridge Ministry of Acadiana, a couple of us attended a weekend workshop that Mo Leveritt was teaching at Desire Street Ministry in New Orleans. Mo was a relatively young warrior who, after graduating from seminary school, marched into the darkest neighborhood in America, the Desire Street Projects. For 15 years or so, he began shining the light of hope, ministering to the generationally poor and unloved, and raising his family.

At this workshop, Mo told us we needed to get on God's Pathway. I asked, "What is God's Pathway?" Mo replied, "God's Pathway is where God is actively working in your community." This was over-my-head (and definitely over-my-heart) at the time, but since I trusted and respected Mo, I committed his revelation to memory.

During the past seven years at the Bridge Ministry of Acadiana, I have daily seen God working in many lives. As volunteers follow Christ across the bridge and into the lives of the unloved poor, I see people on both sides of the bridge being transformed. Friendships are being formed. Love for and from children without fathers has increased. Respect for and from children is growing. Volunteers from over 30 different churches are working across denominational lines. Community trust is increasing across social, economic, and neighborhood divides as businesses and organizations join in. Our community is slowly coming together as friends of God and each other.

After entering the neighborhood, I have learned that God was at work in this neighborhood long before we arrived. Prior to our moving into the neighborhood, there were families who came together weekly and prayed for each other, their churches, and this neighborhood. I learned that one neighbor had the vision years ago for a neighborhood community center for kids in the exact house the Bridge is currently renting. Yes, God was at work in our neighborhood many years before we ever showed up. We could not have seen God's working hands until we relocated into this neighborhood as we did. God has prepared the way, the path, for us to walk. It is just ours to follow.

Seven years ago at Bridge's first Day Camp, I asked our young boys, "What do you want to be when you grew up?" "What do you dream about?" Their empty stares told me they did not comprehend what I was talking about. For them, dreaming was an unknown concept. Last week I was at the Bridge showing a couple of new friends around, when two of these boys, now 17, came in. They introduced themselves, shook hands, looked us in the eye, and took time to chat with us before doing their school work. When asked what they plan to do after graduating from high school, one boy said he plans to go to law school, and the other said he plans to go to ULL and study accounting.

Yes, the many days of tutoring, Boy Scout outings, summer camps, Job Clubs, field trips, music, fishing, camping, Neighborhood Association, adult activities, Bible studies made a difference. With food, fun, and faith, our neighbors came together with us each day and became friends. Building a culture of respect and trust, these two young boys proudly stood before us as a testimony to the success of our faithfully walking along God's Pathway.

After the tour, I reflected back to that day Mo Leveritt said "Get on God's Pathway." I reflected back seven years ago when only 30 percent of the neighborhood kids graduated from high school, and no one in the neighborhood went to college. I remembered the day at summer camp when I asked the boys about their dreams and was stunned by the vacant look in their eyes. Seven years have now passed, and I see these young boys speaking their dreams into a future reality. A future reality that empowers these children, and me, volunteers and our staff to dream dreams of a better tomorrow for our whole community and state. After all, God's Pathway miraculously benefits us all, all the time, and at all levels of our consciousness.

Currently we have had to limit the number of children we serve, and we have created a waiting list. We have dreams and are making plans to increase capacity. We have hopes of increasing the number of kids, neighborhood participation, outreach, volunteers, space, and community investment donations.

In planning for this project, God has been at work. Two acres of land in the neighborhood have been purchased by a generous donor. Architects and contractors have freely offered their services. We have volunteers to do electrical work. Our Neighborhood Association has been raising money for the project. Time required for getting permits from the city has been miraculously cut in half. A quick response for traffic approval has raised everyone's eyebrows. Local investments have begun coming in. And all this without a formal announcement of our full plans.

This increased flow of resources is an example of what one can experience when on God's Pathway. We have seen God working over and over again over the past seven years, as our growth seems to be on steroids. And on God's Pathway we instantly recognize God is in control, not us.

Roughly 2000 years ago, Jesus said: *"Follow Me." (Mat 4:19, NIV) "I am the way, the truth and the life." (John 14:6, NLT)* Jesus Christ humbly moved into our neighborhood to direct us to God's Pathway of love.

"'You must love the Lord your God with all your heart, all your soul, and all your mind.' 38 This is the first and greatest commandment. 39 A second is equally important: 'Love your neighbor as yourself.' 40 The entire law and all the demands of the prophets are based on these two commandments." (Matthew 22:37-40, NLT)

12/09/2010

THE BRIDGE: PAST ~ PRESENT ~ BEYOND

"My grace is sufficient for you, for my power is made perfect in weakness. Therefore I will boast all the more gladly about my weaknesses, So that Christ's power may rest on me." (2 Cor 12:9, NIV)

In the beginning of Bridge Ministry, we were feeling shell-shocked by our little street kids. At the end of every night, the exhausted staff and volunteers would look at each other and silently wonder how long we would last. A volunteer once exclaimed, "I didn't realize how far behind these children are." I told him that we were simply trying to stop the bleeding. Most of our children could not read or do anything past "finger-math," and had never been taught about real life outside the neighborhood.

Some days were so tough, I was weakened to the point that I did not want to go back the next day. Once, a volunteer broke down crying. She admitted that she did not want to come back. The unconscious disobedience and ungratefulness she was experiencing from our children had overwhelmed her. With many prayers, we thank God for giving us His strength, wisdom and grace to lovingly persevere. God proved most faithful as we learned to rely of His strength more and more.

That was then. This is now. This past week my friend Mike called after his first night tutoring at the Bridge. He said, "These kids are smart! I have two post graduate degrees and they were helping me with their homework questions! My only problem was that my time with the children was much too short!"

Recently, one of my friends who grew up on these same streets was at the Bridge before our men's neighborhood Bible study. Bewildered, he asked, "Are these street kids?" Then he instantly answered himself, "I ain't never seen anything like this before. Their momma's don't even get them to act like this." He was amazed to see how bright-eyed, happy, and eager to learn they were.

It is working. Volunteers and staff who daily model what they teach, and pour respect, love and knowledge into these young souls over a long period of time is a model that simply works. Offering love and believing in our children for a long enough time until they believe in themselves simply works.

But beyond where we are, Bridge Ministry of Acadiana desires to do more. We want to educationally and spiritually edify more under-resourced children, and all of Acadiana, on both sides of the bridge. We currently have 60 children signed up at the Bridge with more than 15 on our waiting list. (Yes, we have a waiting list due to our limited space of only 1500 Square Feet.) We currently feel God leading us to go beyond the present and to-take-more-ground.

If you, your friends, and your Church would desire to participate in the fastest growing social exploration and development investment in town, we ask you to consider joining us.

We are most grateful to all our volunteers, social investors, Board of Directors and staff whose shoulders we all stand on in the past, present, and beyond. Thank you ALL. It truly takes a Beloved Village as ours.

03/10/2011

Update: On May 4, 2013 Bridge Ministry of Acadiana celebrated the opening of our two new children's buildings (5,000 sq. ft.) with no debt.

Yea God!!

LEARNING TO WALK (AND KEEPING YOUR BALANCE)

This past weekend I visited my 89-year-old mom. I noticed her balance is getting much worse. She now walks with her hands stretched out touching chairs, or tables, or whatever for added balance as she moves through her home. Last time I took her out to dinner, she hugged the wall as she made her way out to the car. I walked alongside her with her hand lightly leaning on my arm.

When we begin as babies, walking is a major developmental leap, and our parents are often anxious about when we take that first step. It takes most babies about 1,000 hours of practice from the time they pull themselves upright to the time they can walk alone.

When I was a baby, my parents walked in front of me while they held my hands. They also occasionally let go of one hand so that I could experiment and struggle for balance. After I mastered standing-up, I probably bounced from the wall to a chair to the coffee table and to the floor. But soon, after building up the necessary muscles, a baby begins to walk with his hands raised high for balance.

I have a friend who sits on the front row at our church. During praise and worship his big hands are raised high. My friend, unlike the baby, raises his hands high not for physical balance, but for spiritual balance. My friend fearlessly heard God's calling for his life and courageously stood up and walked forward in faith. Motivated by God's deep love and grace given him, he is now empowered to willingly and humbly walk into the life and pain of his neighbor's and become their friend. Volunteering full time at the Bridge, he is not doing "for" but rightly walking "with" and alongside his new friends as they struggle to stand up and walk. In his commitment to walk in Christ's footsteps, he knows he is not able to walk this spiritual journey without God's hand balancing his as he balances another. Through all this, God, our Father, must be anxious for his children to faithfully begin to walk together in unity and purpose.

"There's no way to enter into a place of great need without becoming needy. There's no way to enter into a place of intense dysfunction and disease without requiring healing and cleansing yourself. So even as you administer the gospel, you eventually stand in the need of it."
(Mo Leverett, Desire Street Ministry, New Orleans)

02/01/2011

WITHOUT HOPE

by Kris Newman, Bridge Volunteer

I don't think I have ever been without hope. According to Webster, hope is the feeling that something desired is possible. A few weeks ago, I went door-to-door with three other people in the Four Corners area to do a neighborhood survey. As we were talking to people who lived in the neighborhood, many of them described their lives as having no hope. How did that happen?

I believe that kids are born full of hope ready to trust fully and be loved. Unfortunately, in a moment, hope, trust, and love can be taken away. Dr. Wes Stafford, the president of Compassion International, describes it this way: "A child may be born in poverty, but poverty is never born in a child. The worst aspect of poverty is not the deplorable outward conditions, but rather the erosion and eventual destruction of hope, and therefore dreams."

I have a desire not only to reinstate hope in adults and teens, but I also have a longing to nurture and help grow hope in children. As I have gotten to know some kids from the Bridge neighborhood, I believe these kids have had hope restored. Many people giving up their time to love these kids is making a difference. Love instills hope.

The Bridge children are love sponges. You give them a little love, and they soak it all in. And then, these little love sponges give you unconditional love in return. It blows my mind that my 90 minutes a week can make such a difference. As I sat in the grass reading to the little girls at the Bridge while they were working on my hair, my desire was to be a messenger of hope. Dr. Stafford continues to say, "When a child gives up hope, dreams are forever shattered. With lost dreams goes the potential and ultimate impact that a child might have."

As we continue to plan and prepare to reach out to the children in the Azalea park area, we need to consider how to nurture the dreams of each child and keep hope alive. There are various plans, programs, and strategies we can pursue, but ultimately, the first step to keeping hope alive in children, is to simply love them.

03/28/2011

Update: 08/05/2014 After Kris and her husband and pastor John Newman volunteered at Bridge Ministry of Acadiana, they caught God's vision and began "New Hope" in the fall of 2011. New Hope is located in the under-resourced neighborhood adjacent to the Bridge neighborhood.

LEARNING BY DOING

Jennifer Reynaud, Bridge Ministry of Acadiana's Executive Director, became aware that a couple of our 4th graders were struggling in school this year. During the weekends (her time off) she moved away from their book learning and began to relationally appeal to them through "learning by doing."

In Jennifer's pursuit to fan the flame of learning, she decided to begin a chicken egg business. First, Jennifer had the two children work in our computer lab to discover the different types of chickens. They identified 20 different types. She then asked the kids: "Which hens lay the biggest eggs?"; "What are the colors of their eggs"; "Are the hens better for meat or for laying?"; "Which hens can handle our South Louisiana heat the best?" This moved them to explore deeper. After two weeks they had made charts, compared data, and decided to purchase six Rhode Island Red and six Black Australorp chicks. In short order, they received 12 three-week-old chicks which they began to feed, water, and nurture. But as the chicks grew, they realized that three of them were roosters. They then found someone who would buy one of the roosters, but the prospective purchaser also wanted a hen, so they decided to sell one Black Astralorp hen and one Black Ausralorp rooster. At the local Feed Store, they traded the other two roosters for a bag of feed. So they ended up with five Rhode Island Reds and three Black Australorp laying hens.

Presently their egg production is six eggs per day, and they are selling their eggs for $1.50 per dozen. As Jennifer humorously says about their low price, "we're working on learning the business side, not the get-rich side."

One lady was very nice to them, so the kids thought they would give her some of their eggs. Jennifer explained that while it was good for them to think this way, they could not afford to give away profits if they were to stay in business for very long and that they would have to rethink how to return the lady's kindness in other ways. Through the business, they have had to learn about net profits, operating costs, and future planning. As to operating costs, they figured out that $1.00 per dozen must go back into the business for feed and supplies, and that $.50 per dozen would be their net profit. Jennifer asked them what they wanted to do with the profits, and they decided that they wanted to go to dinner when they had accumulated $20. In this whole loving process, their mental flames have been fanned anew and learning has become not only fun, but exciting, relevant and productive. After all, learning by doing is the best method to develop the human mind.

Learning by doing is also the best method to develop the human heart. It is with hands-on-compassion, not just from a book, that our spiritual gifts and lives are fanned into flames and our hearts grow. In the active process of loving God and our neighbors, our heads, hearts, and hands ultimately meet and mature. If interested, we invite you, your friends, and your church to use the Bridge Ministry of Acadiana as a vehicle to assist in your spiritual development. You can join with us by volunteering, praying, and/or investing.

> *"For this reason I remind you to fan into flame the gift of God, which is in you..." (2 Timothy 1:6, NIV)*

04/15/2011

HEROES OF HOPE

"When people have hope they have the power to change their own destinies and achieve their dreams."
(Connie Sanders, Bridge's first executive director)

When people feel economically and or spiritually powerless and hopeless to effect change in their lives, there then resides a poverty within their souls that ultimately infects the soul of their families, churches, neighborhoods, and community.

In 2003 Bridge Ministry of Acadiana (BMA) rented a house in the center of a forgotten and under-resourced neighborhood. We humbly went door-to-door meeting, listening, and learning from our new neighbors. From these initial meetings, we felt the strong currents of hopelessness in our new neighborhood. We quickly learned these strong rippling currents of hopelessness had also permeated into the lives of the children who were stuck in the "now" with no dreams.

I once asked the children during our first summer camp what they dreamed about, and I shockingly received blank stares in response. Hopeful dreams appeared to be a lost concept, and I now know why 70 percent of our neighborhood had dropped out of high school and none had graduated from college. NOW, eight years later, BMA had four seniors who earned the right to join their 2011 high school graduation class. Three of BMA's four 2011 graduating seniors are now planning to go to college to pursue careers in medicine, accounting and law! Our fourth graduate has dreams to enter the Air Force, and become a pilot. At BMA all four of our graduates have been relationally encouraged and lovingly empowered for the past eight years to hope for and achieve their dreams as designed and purposed for them by God. I might also add, BMA has a huge wave of hopeful children that now dream of following in our graduates' footsteps. There is hope when there is faith and love—especially love.

BMA's 2011 graduates are real heroes to me. We have grown with them and embraced their struggles to heroically swim against the turbulent white water in their lives and neighborhood. Like all heroes, our graduates now inspire our younger future heroes to follow them. The tide is beginning to turn, and BMA's younger children can now envision that they too can do it because of their heroes of hope ahead of them.

BMA's volunteers, investors, interns, staff, and board are real heroes to me also. They too are swimming against the negative currents in our larger community that tell us that there is no hope for "these" neighborhoods. At BMA, this hopelessness is not our experience. After struggling upstream, these heroes are beginning to experience a hope that springs forth when faithful people with resources boldly walk across the "bridge" to become friends with their under-resourced neighbors. Like our graduates who heroically model hope to the BMA children and neighborhood, so too do BMA's heroic volunteers, investors, interns, staff, and board bring hope back into our greater community and beyond. They are our heroes of hope too.

BMA is experiencing God's great hope for our community through all our heroes of hope on both sides of the "bridge." This great hope calls out to us, your friends, your organizations, and your churches to come learn and experience this hope alongside our other heroes. At BMA, we thank God constantly for our faithful and loving investors, volunteers, pray-ers, neighborhood association, interns, children, staff, and Board who together bring great hope to our children, families, neighborhood, community, and beyond. After all, heroes overflow with hope.

"I pray that the God who gives hope will fill you with much joy and peace while you trust in Him. Then your hope will overflow by the power of the Holy Spirit." (Romans 15:13, CEB)

06/08/2011

Update 07/25/2014: One of our High School graduates, Toi James, is attending Community College in Film and Media Studies, while also working the past two years as a staff member at Bridge. As a Staff member, Toi helps lead our middle school children as a tutor, mentor, friend, role model, bible study leader, leads outings, etc. Toi is also Bridge's media and video coordinator. Leadership development is one of our key principles at Bridge Ministry of Acadiana's inner city Christian Community Development mission.

WHEN CAN I COME TO BRIDGE?

As I drove into the Bridge parking lot for our 6 p.m. neighborhood Men's Bible Group, I saw Eric, Bridge Ministry's Elementary Children's Director, sitting on the front porch with a child after Summer Camp. As I got out of my car Eric said, "I just have one more child to get home." Just then a young boy rode into the front yard on his bicycle asking, "Mr. Eric, when can I come to Bridge?" Eric said, "Sorry Ty (not his real name), we don't have any more room in Summer Camp."

It has been a few weeks now and Summer Camp is coming to an end. The Bridge staff is beginning to plan and prepare for the fall 2011 semester. Registration has opened on a first-come-first-serve basis with most of our children's moms rushing to enroll their children as soon as possible. In short order, we had 80 children enroll, but ten live outside our neighborhood and will, regrettably, not be eligible. We also have 14 to 15 children who we know will register, but whose parents have not come to the Bridge yet. Our limit, due mainly to space, will be 73 neighborhood children this fall. This limit is the number of children we believe that we can effectively empower educationally and spiritually, without losing the relational quality of knowing the child, their family, and their teachers.

Our society generally desires and presses for big numbers, which is perceived as having the greatest social impact. As a culture, we are driven by numbers and trained to think that more-is-better and unknowingly devalue the relational power and true influence existing between human beings who rightly care and respect one another. The fact is that when numbers go up, relational quality most often goes down. At the Bridge, we are aware of the tempting social pressures to increase the number of children beyond our true relational capacity just to look good. To effectively increase our number of children in the future, the Bridge must concurrently increase its space and volunteer participation, so our children will always have a place "where everybody knows their name and they are always glad they came and they know all people are the same." *(taken from the "Cheers" TV Theme Song)*

To hear "I do not know you, go away" must be the hardest and most lonely and impoverishing words a person can hear. Jesus hauntingly said to the many at heaven's door, "I do not know you, go away" (Matthew 7, and Luke 13). But Jesus also promised that if we sincerely knock, His door will be graciously opened. As we are designed to desperately seek to be rightly known, loved, respected, and included, can we not also feel and understand this same loneliness and longing in this young boy too?

After eight years at the Bridge, relational bridges have been built across many socio-economic-denominational gaps. The doors of many hearts and minds have been opened along God's pathways. Friendships have developed, and lives have been miraculously transformed on both sides of the proverbial bridge. But in experiencing how faith combined with active love has brought hope to so many, my soul deeply mourns the young soul who asked that day, "Mr. Eric, when can I come to Bridge?" The child is knocking! Let us in our community and as the unified Body of Christ learn to open our doors to all children, as God graciously opens His to us.

"Knock and keep on knocking
and the door shall be opened to you"
(Luke 11:9b, AMP)

07/12/2011

FAMILY FUN DAY IN THE PARK

"Our schools and neighborhoods don't work so well when community bonds slacken."
(Robert Putnum, "Bowling Alone")

Seven years ago the Bridge Neighborhood Association had its first Family Fun Day in the Park in our neighborhood. The Bridge staff and volunteers seemed to do most of the work back then due to a number of issues, one being ourselves. Over the years though, the Neighborhood Association has taken ownership and now provides for the planning, cooking, set-up, food, drinks, etc. The men barbeque burgers and hotdogs. Miss Nola provides the chili. Donations of money, water, soda, chips, and meat are collected from neighbors. There are prizes given away as well as special gifts. All the ladies and men participate and join in the gathering by inviting their neighbors.

Originally we had about 25 kids. This year there were 130+ neighborhood adults and children present, plus over 15 from East Bayou Baptist Church came with their Children's Puppets. The Bayou also wanted to participate by bringing food. The Lafayette Police Department brought out their Armadillo surveillance unit, motorcycles, and horses. Ten officers added value to the gathering by staying the whole day playing with our children and building community and friendships with our neighbors. We played football, basketball, and horseshoes. There was a lot of activity throughout the day on our park's swing sets, jungle-gym and see-saws. Our neighborhood and community were simply taking time to be together as friends.

Building neighborly community over the years has proven to require a committed group of people who regularly come together in friendship over a long period of time. Building trust and friendships has proven to bring a better sense of safety, security, and sense of belonging to our neighborhood (and community), which enhances the well-being of our children. Mr. McZeal, an elderly lifetime resident, recently said, "The neighborhood has improved a lot, Nelson." Added to these neighborhood relationships, faithful folk from outside the neighborhood have intentionally crossed over the socio-economic bridge to humbly enter into friendly relationships with our neighbors and their children to create "bridging relationships." These bonding and bridging relationships create a bonded and well-oiled neighborhood and community. The bonding relationships being built within our neighborhood provide the needed relational glue to bring safety, security, and sense of belonging to the neighborhood; while our community's "bridging" relationships provide the needed relational WD-40 for our community to live alongside each other in harmony and respect.

Ms. Betty commented, "I thought these Family Fun Day in the Park events were for the children, but I know

now they are for us all. When we all come together things just get better." Yes they do Ms. Betty! Yes, they do.

Here's the irony. In our inner-city mission at the Bridge, we encourage our neighbors to regularly come together in friendship so they will become stronger together than they will alone and separate. We do this because we know this to be true.

Many books, like *Bowling Alone,* and much practical research attest to these relational truths, as does the Bible. But, sometimes what we know to be true, we, ironically, do not do ourselves on the other side of the bridge. We talk it, but do not do it. This is especially true within the Body of Christ which is specifically commanded to love and respect each other and become the irresistible light on the hill. We know it is the right thing to do, but for many reasons we have no will to do it. Please join me in prayer for the Body of Christ in Lafayette to respectfully come together as our Bridge Neighborhood Association's Family Fun Day in the Park so aptly models for us all to do.

"I am giving you a new commandment: Love each other. Just as I have loved you, you should love each other."
(John 13:34, NLT)

10/26/2011

AN OLD MAN AND A BOY

"Teach these things and make sure everyone learns them well. [12] Don't let anyone think little of you because you are young. Be their ideal; let them follow the way you teach and live; be a pattern for them in your love, your faith, and your clean thoughts."
(1 Timothy 4:11-12, TLB)

The other night I was getting ready for our neighborhood Men's 100X Bible Study when the door opened and a 6'4" young man walked in and looked at me with a knowing smile. My heart leaped as my mind flashed back nine years ago when this young man was ten.

He came over and hugged me. He began telling me that he had thought of me often and wanted to tell me how much he appreciated us being there every day for them at the Bridge. He said that he would not be where he is today without us.

Last week he had attended the Bridge High School Bible study at our Youth Coordinator's house. During the Bible study, he said he wanted to cry remembering all our Bible Studies, tutoring, swimming, fishing trips, etc. over the years.

I then flashed back to our first summer camp nine years ago, where I asked him and nine other boys what they wanted to be when they grew up. Their silent response and blank stares startled me as I saw that they had no dreams. But a year later, I remember this young boy telling me that he wanted to become a lawyer someday. He had a dream! So, I looked up and asked the tall young man in front of me now, "Are you working on becoming a lawyer?" With his great smile, he said, "Yes."

I told him that I remembered at the funeral of a Youth Coordinator, Illinois Thomas, how impressed I was when he, out of our 30 children, boldly stood up in front of a few hundred people that he did not know. He spoke about this man he had respected, loved, and lost. With a presence beyond his 12 years, he spoke from his heart and with clarity about Illinois. I knew then that this young man, who had captured my heart, was going to be an extra special man someday. I was fighting back tears just looking at him now. I told him he was going to be a very good lawyer, but more importantly a great man, husband, father, and community leader. I told him how proud I was of him, and that I loved him. I told him that he had a good mind and a caring heart, and a gift for speaking... plus a great sense of humor too! "God has blessed you to bless others."

Again, he thanked me, and I thanked him. With a quick and curious look, he questioned why I had thanked him. I explained that an older man, like myself, needs a boy close to him, like yourself, so as to have meaning and purpose in life. I told him that us older guys need you younger guys, as much or more than you younger guys need us older guys. "You see my young friend, through you God has enlarged my heart and brought me closer to Himself. Thank you!" Just an old man and a boy. Simple, yet powerful and profound.

I thank all the older men in my life who admired and loved me. Thanks for seeing past the boy in front of you and seeing the future man I could and would become. I wish you were alive today, so I could tell you what this capable and caring young man had just told me. May God bless those young boys among us who have no admiring and loving men in their lives. Lord, let your face shine on them all in our community and beyond.

"Train up a child in the way he should go and in keeping with his individual gift or bent, and when he is old he will not depart from it." (Proverbs 22:6, AMP)

07/25/2011

Update, 07/25/2014: This young man is continuing his undergraduate work at University of Lafayette Louisiana. He works in a local law office gaining experience and shadowing lawyers and good men.

THE SYMPHONY

"From Him the whole body, joined and held together by every supporting ligament, grows and builds itself up in love, as each part does its work."
(Ephesians 4:16, NIV)

I recently re-united with an old friend in Houston after many years. Steve, a world renowned baritone and professor of music at William Patterson University in New Jersey, was contracted to sing with the Houston Symphony last week. My wife and I drove over for the day.

Steve had told me that he cannot remember not singing, as his father was a music professor at Princeton and raised Steve in a most fertile musical soil. Music has been God's gift that has flowed from Steve's father down to Steve. God's gifts, as designed, continue to flow from Steve and into his pupils, audiences, and other symphonies worldwide.

As I watched Steve in front of the 200 plus people in the Houston orchestra and the 200 plus people in their choir, I realized that we were sitting in front of a very accomplished and gifted assembly of people. Out of curiosity, I applied what is known as the "10,000 Hour Rule" which basically states that 10,000 hours of training is required for a person to become accomplished and competent in their professional field. With approximately 400 people on stage this would be equivalent to a combined four million hours of individual struggles, diligent work, and perseverance. Calculating a 40-hour training week per performer is equivalent to a total of 100,000 weeks, or about 2,000 cumulative years of full-time (mostly unpaid) training.

Recognizing this fact that there was 2,000 years of experience represented on stage is most humbling indeed. Many hours of training are required for a person to become independent and self-sufficient, and many more hours are required for a competent person to become conscious of their inter-dependency within our human symphony.

If a group of accomplished musicians independently played their music without a care for the other musicians, nothing more than irritating noise would come forth, defeating their desired purpose to enhance the flow of their gifts of music to others. Yet when the musicians respectfully come together in unity around their desired purpose and diverse talents, their music takes on a big and powerful sound that can never be produced independently—only together.

At the Bridge, we see God's gifts of grace flowing daily within our neighborhood and across the bridge into our beloved community through a symphony of competent and caring people. People that empower other people create the fertile soil for their neighborhoods, families, and children to thrive. In building these relational bridges, God's blessings are now able to flow between neighbors, volunteers, and supporters from over 30 different churches within the Body of Christ and beyond for the mutual benefit of all.

This Thanksgiving, let us give thanks to God from whom all our many blessings flow. His blessings flow down like a river into our community, neighborhoods, our families, ourselves, and into the hearts and minds of our children. We are more than thankful for God's blessings through His beloved symphony of faithful people that come together as one at the Bridge. Praise be to God. Grace and Peace to you, your families, and friends this Thanksgiving week. We thank you all for being you!

"Praise God, from Whom all blessings flow"
(Thomas Ken, 1674)

11/22/2011

DO GOOD, FEEL GOOD

I remember asking God, "What have you brought to us in Ed (changed name)?" Ed showed up at the Bridge as a grumpy and demanding old cuss. I would love to say that he is not that way now, but that would be stretching the truth a bit. Like my wife says of me, "Nelson's getting better," and so is Ed. Some of the men have commented that Ed is softening up, and he has even been caught laughing.

Ed is elderly, and his friends in the neighborhood all watch out for him. He lives in a small shotgun house across the street from where the "Slab" used to be. The Slab was widely known as the epicenter for drug trafficking and drinking when we first moved into this under-resourced Lafayette neighborhood in 2003.

About a year ago the Bridge Men's Bible Study group came together in the middle of winter to replace Ed's front porch and a 3' x 4' rotten hole in his bedroom floor where he had laid a board to walk across. Recently, our neighborhood men planned another workday at Ed's house. His bathroom floor had rotted out under the toilet. His toilet was propped up with a stick and teetering on the pipe below.

The men's group developed a plan. Two men had parts from ¾" plywood sheets for his flooring. I had an electric saw and other tools. A couple of men even had strong backs that we needed desperately. So we met at Ed's this past Saturday to fix his bathroom flooring and plumbing. As luck would have it, a man showed up who actually knew what he was doing. At the end of the job, as before, we felt good. Real good.

I know we say it is more blessed to give than receive, but is it really? Think about the people you know who are habitually kind. They are not kind to prove that giving and blessings go together. They seem to do what they do because they love to. Their habits of kindness have become their character. They embody this character of kindness in order to serve others that are most often not able to do for themselves. They seem to have a deep sense and consistent love for humanity.

If you are fortunate to know one of these great souls, you will notice that they all have a certain joy about them—a deep attractive joy that inspires you "up" not "down." Every time you leave one of these unique human beings you feel empowered and filled up, not depleted. And we look forward to being with them again. You may have noted that many of these people happen to live a very long life too. Their common denominator is that they find peace and joy in loving, and being kind. Life is not about them. Their lives are living proof that it is truly more blessed to give than receive. They are the model of God's spiritual genius at work. They like people.

But what does science say about "doing good"? Do "do-gooders" experience higher levels of mental well-being, physical health, emotional health, spiritual health? Increasingly, scientists are beginning to study those who habitually "do good."

From the International Encyclopedia of the Social

Sciences: "We should not be surprised to learn that people feel good when they do good. Group selection theory in evolution shows that groups that are strong in internal altruism have a selective advantage over other groups (Sober and Wilson 1998). Thus, it makes evolutionary sense that helping behavior within groups would be connected with stimulating feelings of well-being." (Bachner-Melman et al. 2005)

"Well-being" is characterized as feeling hopeful, happy, and good about oneself, as well as energetic and connected to others. In an early study that compared retirees over age 65 who volunteered with those who did not, volunteers scored significantly higher in life satisfaction and will to live, and had fewer symptoms of depression, anxiety, and somatization (Hunter and Lin 1981).

More recent studies confirm an association between altruistic activities and well-being and life satisfaction in older adults (Dulin and Hill 2003; Liang et al. 2001; Morrow-Howell et al. 2003). Midlarsky (1991) found five benefits to older adults who engage in altruistic behavior: enhanced social integration; distraction from the agent's own problems; enhanced meaningfulness; increased perception of self-efficacy and competence; and improved mood and/or more physically active lifestyle. Midlarsky and Kahana (1994) associated adult altruism—that is, voluntary behavior that is "motivated by concern for the welfare of the other, rather than by anticipation of rewards," with improved morale and self-esteem, positive affect, and well-being. The mental health benefits of giving in the form of volunteerism include fewer depressive symptoms (Musick and Wilson

2003) and greater happiness and well-being (Krueger et al. 2001).

In his book *The Happiness Hypothesis* (2006), Jonathan Haidt, a social psychologist at the University of Virginia, discusses great ancient ideas about human flourishing—that is, what makes for a happy and meaningful human life. Haidt explains how the human system of attachment has evolved and how important it is to our successful development, emphasizing Émile Durkheim's idea that the ties, bonds, and obligations of our lives are actually mentally and physically good for us. "Helping others provides more benefits than receiving help; and, strong social relationships increase immunity, speed healing, and reduce the risks of depression." (Haidt 2006). (quoted from "Generosity/Selfishness;" *International Encyclopedia of the Social Sciences*, 2008; http://www.encyclopedia.com/doc/1G2-3045300912.html)

So, all the recent research and even our personal experiences point to our soul's designed purpose to: "Do Good, Feel Good." In this we thank God for old grumpy Ed and each other!

"Then your light will break forth like the dawn,
and your healing will quickly appear"
(Isa 58:8a, NIV)

01/17/2012

IRRITATIONS

"We love because He first loved us."
(1 John 4:19, NIV)

When the Bridge moved into the neighborhood eight years ago, most of the children could not read or do their own homework. The neighborhood high school dropout rate was 70 percent.

Presently, I have begun working with the middle school children during our "Homework Help" on Mondays after school. After a few years of absence from this hands-on work with the children, I am very encouraged to see that now the middle-schoolers have the ability to do their own homework and need only a little help and encouragement. This was definitely not the case eight years ago. Something has changed.

Last Monday, I became irritated with one of the little girls, who was distracted by every little thing. The young boy next to her stayed focused and did his work, but she was checking out every person, movement, and sound. Body language speaks very loudly in the inner-city, so her focus was everywhere except doing her school work. My job was, I thought, to encourage her to stay focused on her work even after her long day at school, but she seemed to be ignoring my presence. Without much love or patience, I admit, I wanted to say, "Can't you see what I am trying to do here for you?"

Just before 5 p.m., Joel, our middle school coordinator, came in and told the children to pack-up their books and get ready for the next activity. The children began to move and talk with each other. I tried to ask them about Mardi Gras week, but I was ignored as though I was not even present. I guess that did it, because I have been reflecting on this irritation for a week now. In my prayers I asked God to help this girl focus on her school work and even become more respectful, but God had something else in mind. In my prayers and reflections His word and Spirit began revealing that I needed to change first.

A few days later, as I was praying, an ambulance shrieked down my street. I disrespectfully dropped out of prayer with God and rushed to the window. Afterwards, I began half-heartedly praying, but I was again distracted by the worries of the day and things that "I" needed to do. Like the little girl, my focus was on everything, but what was important. "Heck, I'm more distracted than the little girl," I realized. What I found irritating about the little girl's relationship to me, I was doing in my relationship with God. God was probably saying to me: "Can't you see that this is not so much about her head, but your heart Nelson? This child will not care about what you KNOW until she knows you first CARE. She will hear and focus better when your heart is clear and full. Just as I loved you first, you must love her first." (1 John 4:19).

Wow! Who, but this inner-city child, can God so easily mirror myself in? In her need, I saw my need. In this revelation, I now wholeheartedly pray for us both, and now I look forward to seeing her instead of dreading her. My job and responsibility is to first show this child that I care, because the fact is Christ first cared for me, and I have to believe He grins down on us when we do the same.

Fascinatingly, the next time I sat with her was a most beautiful experience that gave me a small taste of God's faithfulness. We still have a long way to go, but the path is clearer. Something gets changed at Bridge, and that something is hearts and (then) minds—and that being on both sides of the bridge.

During the following weeks, I experienced my heart in prayer drastically changing toward the little girl, and experienced the little girl's attitudes begin changing toward me. God's antidote to my irritations was surely experienced on the other side through prayer and love.

"I urge you, brothers and sisters, by our Lord Jesus Christ
and by the love of the Spirit, to join me in my struggle
by praying to God for me."
(Romans 15:30, NIV)

02/22/2012

SHOWING GOD'S LOVING-KINDNESS

"Love Builds Up" (1 Corinthians 8:1b, NIV)

I grew up next door to my Great Aunt Myrtle Rodgers, who was always there for us. Years later, my mom visited Grand Myrt, who then had Alzheimer's disease. During that visit Grand Myrt weakly said to my mom, "I don't know you, but I know you are someone who is kind and cares about me."

Loving Kindness is not so easily and quickly measured as most things in our lives are measured. Yet, our human need for kindness is not easily forgotten, even for those with little to no memory. For the truth is that those with very little memory do remember kindness. Those who are blind can see kindness. The deaf can actually hear kindness. People who are unfairly seen as unworthy in our community can see their worthiness in the kindness shown to them by others. People who are poor and oppressed are truly set free and empowered through kind and loving acts. Simply said, our human dignity, and our society, is built up and sustained by right and loving kindness.

Maybe this New Year is our appointed time to learn how to better act in loving-kindness that causes no further dependency or harm and that truly build others up. It's a time to learn to not continually do "for" another person, which can cause dependency, but to rightly and lovingly do "with" another person, which releases and develops a person to become spiritually and economically whole.

And, it is through our right show of kindness that we better see, hear, and remember our Lord and those who rightly showed us the kindness that built us up. In remembrance I thank God for the many before us, like my Grand Myrt, who rightly showed the loving kindness that built up both my mind and heart as a child. May we return God's loving kindness that releases, develops, and empowers us and our neighbor's children this coming year and beyond.

The Spirit of the Lord is on Me. He has put His hand on Me to preach the Good News to poor people. He has sent Me to heal those with a sad heart. He has sent Me to tell those who are being held that they can go free. He has sent Me to make the blind to see and to free those who are held because of trouble. 19 He sent Me to tell of the time when men can receive favor with the Lord." (Luke 4:18-19, NLV)

12/28/2012

DE'VANTE

"Train up a child in the way he should go [And, in keeping with his individual gift or bent], and when he is old he will not depart from it."(Proverbs 22:6, AMP)

I met De'vante in 2003. He was among the very first children who came to Bridge Ministry. He was 9-years-old and about 4'10" then. Today, he's 6'4" and 19-years-old.

I remember our first summer camp when I asked the ten boys in front of me, "What do you dream about becoming in life?" I was met with blank stares. This startled me as I realized that they did not dream about the future. Well, De'vante did have a dream. He came to me later and said, "Mr. Nelson, I want to become a lawyer."

He now tells me that he first met people who were lawyers at Bridge, people who were volunteering on a regular basis and who became his role models. At Bridge he remembers hearing that lawyers, as a profession, represented more volunteers, donors, and prayers than any other profession at Bridge. These lawyers' noble ways were obviously very attractive to young De'vante. He said, "Their regular presence in my life made becoming a lawyer a realistic possibility for me." This was an enlightening revelation and vision for young De'vante who had previously never known an attorney, and especially never known one as a friend until Bridge moved into the neighborhood.

During the coming years, I watched De'vante grow in statue and character. I watched him struggle in math and conquer it. With an aching heart I watched him boldly stand up at the funeral of our Children Director to speak to a few hundred people about his lost friend and mentor, Mr. Illinois. I also admired his sense of humor even when his humor got ahead of him in our Bible Studies and elsewhere.

He was always lovingly obedient to his Grandmother, even when she would not allow him to go swimming with our other children. For two summers he patiently and pleasantly sat on the side of the pool while his friends swam and played. I remember after a number of trips to persuade his Grandmother to allow De'vante to swim, Illinois finally received a "yes" from her. That was a big day undergirded with her growing trust in us.

Then, one day during High School, De'Vante walked into the Bridge changed, as many of our children have done and will do. He still had his wonderful sense of humor, but he had left many of the childish middle school ways behind. In the days since I have begun seeing more and more of the man he is designed by God to become.

De'Vante says he was introduced to our Lord Jesus Christ at Bridge, but had somehow become disconnected in the past year. He heard through his friend Toi that Mr. Jason, Bridge's Youth Coordinator, had a Bible Study at his house in the neighborhood. He began attending. De'vante even began going to church with Jason. He experienced the loving community of this church and knew this love was the "real deal." De'vante says, "The people at Jason's church don't just talk it, they really live it. One man even invited me to go to lunch with him! The spiritual aspect of my life is the biggest part now and should be stated above all else." He now feels connected not only with our Lord, but also in a church community alongside friends.

Today, De'Vante is attending the University of Louisiana Lafayette studying Criminal Justice with a Minor in English. He works at CVS to defray his expenses. De'vante's dream to become an attorney is still clearly in sight. I see him not only becoming a very capable attorney, but a caring one too. Just like the volunteering attorneys he aspired to become ten years ago as a child, De'vante will become that same competent and caring leader and role model to many other young people beyond his practice of law. The daily development of this young man's mind and heart reflects Bridge's goals to wholistically develop and empower lives mentally and spiritually and to raise up indigenous leaders who will rightly and caringly pass-the-baton of leadership to the next generation and their children.

"A good leader motivates, doesn't mislead, doesn't exploit. God cares about honesty in the workplace; your business is his business. Good leaders abhor wrongdoing of all kinds; sound leadership has a moral foundation. Good leaders cultivate honest speech; they love advisors who tell them the truth. An intemperate leader wreaks havoc in lives; you're smart to stay clear of someone like that. Good-tempered leaders invigorate lives; they're like spring rain and sunshine." (Prov. 16:10-15, MSG)

04/01/2013

BACK PACK PALS

by Bob Lupton
FCS Urban Ministries, Atlanta, Ga.

Dear Bob:

We have started a Back Pack Pals Program (kids that are hungry will get a back pack of food for the weekend). We have heard from teachers that this has helped so many kids. They are improving with discipline issues, academics, and parent/teacher relationships. I was wondering your thoughts on this type of program, and how we can adjust it so that it is NOT a handout or "entitlement" situation? We have so many church members that are active in this ministry, we DON'T want to just kill it – there might be some blow back. How can we adjust it so that it is more in line with the philosophy you espouse?

Donna

Dear Donna:

I understand the appeal of the back pack food program. Hungry children always touch the hearts of compassionate people. And the back pack concept is such an easy image to convey. All you need is one moving story of a neglected child, and it becomes a highly marketable approach. Easy to organize and expedite.

But take a quick glimpse behind the scenes at the home life of the child and the need immediately becomes more complicated. A single mom struggling with addiction, predatory men coming in and out the home, food stamps being bartered for cigarettes and alcohol, back pack food being used to support a destructive lifestyle. Or perhaps the situation is not quite this dire. Perhaps it is a mother, probably single, who is working two jobs to support her family but must leave her children unsupervised much of the time. She may be doing her best to provide, being as responsible as she is able, but the influences of the street constantly lure her kids into unwholesome activities. Back pack food supplements are appreciated, but they do not address the real pressures she is facing.

What every child needs most in life is a stable home with two effective parents. In our inner-cities, one effective parent is usually optimal. Food security, as important as it may be, does not compare with the need for a responsible parent. Our society provides a food safety net for children – free meals at school and food stamps for the family. Such entitlements do encourage dependency, but are probably necessary when families face difficult economic times. But when the crisis passes, when parents are back at work, when the back rent is caught up, this is the time for development – not continued emergency assistance. Struggling parents need a plan, a coach, a training program, a better job, hope. And kids need the benefit of heartened parents. Does a back pack food program offer this? I suspect not.

The only way to responsibly assess the need for

additional supplemental weekend food is to have personal involvement with the family. Teachers can give anecdotal reports on a few children, usually without much depth. School social workers sometimes have a better feel for home life realities. After-school programs run by churches and non-profits often have the best insight. The more personal time invested with a child and his or her family the more accurate the picture. The key to effective service, of course, is to accurately assess the need, then apply the appropriate remedy. A broad brush, indiscriminate distribution of resources without in-person knowledge of need, is not only irresponsible, it may actually be harmful.

So what to do with your Back Pack Pals Program? I guess you first have to ask: "Who is this program for?" I know it seems so compassionate, so right, so biblical. But it is unexamined charity. In order to verify that it is transformative rather than toxic, due diligence must be conducted to determine the downstream impact. Anecdotal reports from teachers are insufficient. Homes and families must be visited, personal relationships must be forged, insights must be gained to determine priority needs and appropriate actions. Obviously, this cannot be done en masse. Or quickly. It is personal work. It does not lend itself to large numbers. It will likely require trustworthy partners on the ground who will serve as guides. And it will likely call for engagement far more involved than food collection and distribution.

Which brings me back to my earlier question: "Who is this program for?" I know how we Americans love to design efficient systems that yield big results. And we're good at it. That's why programs like Back Pack Pals are so appealing to us. But effective service among the poor is neither efficient nor large-scale. Effective service is relational. We might take the position that the teachers have the relationship with the kids and Book Bag Buddies is serving the poor by supporting the teachers. Perhaps. But teachers are not social workers. They are about developing young minds, not intervening in family affairs. And if a child's greatest need is a stable home and an effective parent, then Back Pack Pals as currently structured does not go to that need. Further, without accountability there is no assurance that the donations are benefitting the intended recipients. The program is an emergency response to a chronic poverty need. Development, not donations, is what a chronic situation calls for.

So how could the program be modified to a more developmental approach? A food co-op for parents might be one approach. Parents could purchase donated food, thus increasing the buying power of their food dollar while preserving their dignity – and supporting their responsibility as providers for their families. Kids could do extra duties around the school to earn their back packs. Back packs could become rewards for performance and achievements. Delicate business perhaps, but it would certainly reveal just how important the food is to them. To the extent that there is mutual exchange in the program, to that degree there is dignity and accountability.

Responsible charity follows this progression: immediate care with a future plan; emergency relief with responsible development; short term intervention with long term involvement; heart responses with engaged minds. If we do it right we will see the following outcomes: human dignity is enhanced (mutual exchange); trusting relationships grow (accountability over time); self-sufficiency increases (employment, self-reliance).

I hope this helps,

Bob

04/25/2013

NOTE: Robert Lupton is founder of FCS Urban Ministries in Atlanta. His monthly newsletter is called "Urban Perspectives" (http://fcsministries.org/urban-perspectives/). I recommend all his books, especially *Theirs Is The Kingdom*, *Compassion, Justice and the Christian Life*, and *Toxic Charity*.

Thank you Bob!

OUR FATHER

This past week I lost my dear mother of 91 plus years. Since her passing, I have realized how I had taken for granted her tremendous influence in my life.

I am finding myself shocked in the different ways that I am constantly reminded of her salient influence in my life. Even in the bathroom I am reminded of her "proper" way to place toilet paper on the roller! I am reminded of her when I pick up a fork, or when I am not sitting up straight. In social and workplace situations, I am reminded of the manners and etiquette she diligently taught me over many years. She taught me how to be grateful and modeled how to love without judging. I am reminded of the 10,000 habits developed through 500,000 reminders that she instilled in me, which habits have now become a big part of my character. Bottom line, I am shocked to see how much she has influenced me and now lives in me. As I presently come and go through the day, she truly lives in me.

It has been 31 years since Dad's passing, and I find myself constantly remembering his influential ways too. Remembering and doing as he taught me through his humble sacrificial and committed actions of loving God, family, and others. Yes, I am shocked to see how he too lives in me today. I hope that when one looks at me, they may someday see my dad. It seems we simply become who and what we love. What we reflect is the true legacy of our loving relationships.

At Bridge Ministry of Acadiana, we have found that the vast majority of our children come to us with no fathers living with them. They have not experienced knowing a father's loving faithfulness, and trustworthiness. Many have not experienced the safety and security of their father's encouraging touch and presence in their lives. Most of our children have never heard that God loves them dearly. The Bridge community is there to reflect Our Father's love for his children in ways they will see, so they will know Him and allow Him to live in them too.

This Fatherly void in our children, or even us, cries out to be filled by something. As Phillip asked Jesus: *"Lord, show us the Father [cause us to see the Father—that is all we ask]; then we shall be satisfied. (John 14:8 AMP)*

Jesus answered Phillip: *"...Anyone who has seen me has seen the Father... I am in the Father, and that the Father is in me ... it is the Father, living in me, who is doing his work. Believe me when I say that I am in the Father and the Father is in me; or at least believe on the evidence of the works themselves. I will not leave you as orphans; I will come to you." (John 14:9-11, 18, NIV)*

Jesus loves his Father and thus lovingly reflects His Father to us. His Father lives in Him, as He lives in His Father. Love is most influential and marvelous, as we truly do become what we love and who we love.

Please pray for our children to choose to love the right things in life. Our Father's promise is that we, who choose to love Him, need not remain fatherless, fearful, and alone anymore. Let us all faithfully, gratefully, and truthfully pray in Him: "*OUR Father…*" *(Mat 6:9, NIV).*

06/14/2013

DESTINY

Leadership development is a very high value at Bridge Ministry of Acadiana. Our dream is to raise up indigenous neighborhood leaders who will one day put us out of business. We envision our children not only rightly leading others one day, but also holistically leading their future whole families too.

As trees take time to mature and produce significant fruit, our maturing future leaders will take time too. Leadership development at Bridge is concerned with both educational development and character development. What character model do we follow? We simply ask our children to follow us as we in faith follow our Lord. He is Bridge's model for character and leadership.

Character, not IQ, is the best predictor of a successful, purposeful, and joy-filled life that will reflect our right relationships with God, self, and others. Our challenge at Bridge is to build these good character traits and habits in our children that will persist against all of life's storms and have the self-control to not act in destructive ways, the faith to stay on the right path when the world is constantly calling you down, and remain conscientious and responsible, caring and respectful, encouraging others, possessing emotional control, honesty, integrity, a strong work ethic, generosity, gratefulness, trustworthiness, knowing social and workplace rules of etiquette, etc. These are all learned habits that will become our character that defines us.

Most often our society does not see our children or offer leadership roles to our children from under-resourced neighborhoods. One of Bridge's 5th graders is a quiet girl, who many people would not see as a leader. Most would pass over her, not affirming the image of our Lord and Leader innate in her. But Mrs. Erin, our Elementary Director, began asking this young quiet girl to help her with the daily snacks. Mrs. Erin asked her to take a survey of the healthy snacks that the elementary children desired. She came back with her list, which included Trail Mix. It was explained to her that this might not work because the kids throw the raisins on the ground. They then step on the raisins, which are then tracked back into the new buildings on their shoes, which the children in their daily chores must clean and vacuum every day. The young girl quickly made the decision to take the trail mix off their desired snack list.

This girl also puts the snacks out every day and gets them ready for her friends, and she is in charge of deciding the next week's snacks too. She is taking great pride in doing her job well. This builds her character in taking responsibility, taking action, being conscientious, being responsive to others and serving her friends and her leader, Mrs. Erin. By being invited into a leadership role, she can begin to grow into the true servant leader that God has designed her to become. Many times we need to offer leadership roles to our young children who can become our future influential leaders in our neighborhoods, community, and beyond.

Another young girl came to us with anger issues.

She constantly fired back at others with no self-control or respect for others or herself. She would become very destructive in her reactions, especially when her little brother was being picked on. While protecting her little brother is a good thing, her manner of protection was abusive and destructive. Ms. Joel, our Middle School Director, has been mentoring and disciplining her for over two years to show her better options and respectful ways to act. Ms. Joel is lovingly teaching her how to be more influential in building others up, and not tearing them down with destructive behavior. She is doing this while providing the relational time and space for her to openly reflect and think about her actions too. She is offered biblical stories and positive options that give her not only a new vision of how to act, but also a truer vision of who she is created in God to be. This young girl is not only learning that she is loved, but that she is able to love others too. This past week, in an instance where she would normally have had one of her attacks, she simply looked over at Ms. Joel and gave her a knowing nod. She is learning to become a leader, and her character is beginning to reflect this growth. This is only a small step in the 10,000 steps that we will walk alongside this young girl to build her up, as Christ builds us up too.

Wholeness and Leadership development is a high value at Bridge, and we see every one of our children as future leaders in their families and our community. At the core of our leadership development is the development of good character through experiential faithful habits. Yes, education is important, but it is the good qualities of our character that are most predictive of a successful, joy-filled, and abundant life that will attract others. It is our good character habits that will determine our destinies. The destiny of our Bridge children in Christ is most bright indeed.

It does not take just any kind of village to raise a child, but it does take a Beloved Community with good character to model and raise-up our children.

"So don't lose a minute in building on what you've been given, complementing your basic faith with good character, spiritual understanding, alert discipline, passionate patience, reverent wonder, warm friendliness, and generous love, each dimension fitting into and developing the others. With these qualities active and growing in your lives, no grass will grow under your feet, no day will pass without its reward as you mature in your experience of our Master Jesus." (2 Peter 1:5-8, MSG)

11/01/2013

HEAVY LIFTING

"Each person should remain in the situation They were in when God called them."
(1 Cor 7:20, NIV)

I sat in my friend's office watching him write a generous check to Bridge Ministry of Acadiana. He stopped. He looked up at me and said, "I wish I could do more than just write a check." I said, "What you do is very important." He said, "No, you all do the heavy lifting."

Why didn't I have a more convincing and reassuring reply? I had struggled for years to know how to intimately connect my friends' daily work to their kingdom callings at Bridge and beyond. My problem was that I had not yet made the faith and work connection myself. My friend made me realize that I did not have a holistic theology of work either. I was not seeing our work as God sees it.

I remember having this disconnected feeling at church. One Sunday, the short-term mission teams were asked to stand up while the whole congregation rightly prayed over them. After many years of praying over these overseas mission teams, the church has inadvertently established a higher value for the short-term missions than for people entering into their work place mission field every Monday morning. The "ALL" in *"Go into all the world" (Mark 16:15)* did not seem to include the workplace or our community. I remember when I left church that Sunday, I disconnectedly thought, "Ugh, tomorrow is Monday and back to the grind." I obviously had no vision or understanding of my larger kingdom calling through my vocation.

At the time I did not know that I did not know. I did not know that I had no holistic vision for the theology of work. I had never been taught how my work fit into God's Kingdom agenda every day and had relevance. My spheres of work and spirituality were separate and different, like my Sundays and Mondays. But, I began to see that this dichotomy was not of God's making. By trying to understand the theology of work I began to see how the spiritual and physical are the same to God.

As one and the same, what would it look like if in our churches on Sunday we routinely asked our workers and volunteers to stand up, as we raised them up, regularly valued and affirmed them, fervently prayed over and then commissioned them to boldly go inflict love into their work-places. To intentionally commission them to humbly and respectfully go and lift burdens, close gaps, and make whole what has been broken; to become "the light of the world" (Matt 5:14, NIV) where they are already.

My friend said, "I wish I could do more…" Without work there is no economy. Without work there is no church to gather together and worship in. Without work there is no mission or missionaries. Without work society and families fall apart. Without work there are no schools. Without work there is no better way to mature good character. Without work there is no purpose, joy, and meaning in life. Without work people lose dignity, do not eat, and die.

I have wondered "What is the theology of work?" "How does God see our work?" Briefly stated, we are created in the image of God. God's image in us is spiritual and foundational to our human dignity, and it's the place to start. We are spiritual beings. God worked, and gave work to man before the "Fall." Work, as designed by God, is His gift to us for our wholeness sake. Jesus, our model, worked and was known not just as a working rabbi, but as a carpenter. Jesus was surrounded by and followed by people who worked: fishermen, farmers, tax collectors, doctors, shepherds, soldiers, and tentmakers. Jesus taught mostly about the Kingdom of God by speaking in terms of work: a working farmer, a working king, a merchant, fishermen, sowers and harvesters, bakers, landowner and vine growers, labors in a vineyard, etc. Jesus, our great teacher, made the Kingdom of God simpler for people to comprehend by relating their work to his Kingdom teachings.

A holistic theology of work allows us to envision how our faith and work are integrated. The theology of work helps to interdependently weave God, self, neighbor, family, and creation together as one. Work is highly individual, social, and sacred all at the same time.

Mankind was given dominion over the earth to be a steward of God's good creation through work. Work is sacred. As designed by God, work images our Creator. Work provides mankind with the realization of our humanity; fulfills our calling (within God's Will); develops habits of ethical and moral behavior; and corresponds to, expresses, and increases the dignity of mankind.

Working habits create and develop many virtuous character traits: industriousness, excellence, perseverance, trust, loyalty, creativity, responsibility, respect, reliability, self-control, contentment, joy, manners, fairness, justice, honesty, generosity, resilience, etc.

Giving a person a job is our highest form of charity. Work is mission. Work is essential to a full life and shalom. The fact is that God highly values you and your work. (By the way, for those who volunteer, your volunteering is work too). Your work is most sacred. Your work is the heavy lifting!

"Vocational stewardship (the intentional deployment of our workplace knowledge, skills, platforms, investments (and networks) provides us a way to advance the Kingdom for our community's transformation." (*Kingdom Calling* by Dr. Amy Sherman)

At Bridge we thank God for you and your work. You are highly valued in God's Kingdom agenda "on earth as it is in heaven."

BRIDGE THANKS YOU FOR YOUR SACRED WORK AND YOUR HEAVY LIFTING!

"And let the beauty of the Lord our God be upon us, and establish the work of our hands for us; Yes, establish the work of our hands."
(Psalm 90:17, NIV)

11/08/2013

THE THIRD & FOURTH WORLDS

"When the foundations are being destroyed,
What can the righteous do?"
(Psalm 11:3, NIV)

Kollie Jallah, a visiting pastor and County Director with Change Agent Networks in Liberia, asked to come see the Bridge Ministry of Acadiana. His request was a most unique request, especially coming from a third-world tourist from Africa. This was a new experience for us, and for him.

As I drove Kollie through our Bridge neighborhood, I heard him groan, and then in bewilderment he said, "If I were to instantly appear here in this neighborhood, I would have never guessed that I was in America." Thus, our conversations began...

Spending part of two days together, we learned a lot about each other, our cultures, our histories, and ourselves. Kollie lived through Liberia's 14 year Civil War. The seeds of this Liberian conflict were originally sown in the 1600's-1800's slave trade with America. The seeds were further sown by an American group, which established Liberia as a nationalized state in 1847 by our freed American slaves, the Americo-Liberians. This state was unfortunately established by the use of force to sustain the Americo-Liberian settlers' hegemony.

The established nationalized state immediately divided Liberian natives and the newly freed American slave settlers. The obvious issue associated with America's Civil War was closely woven into Liberia's historic unrest and recent civil war. Liberia's Civil War broke out between 1989-2003. Over 250,000 people were killed. Many, like Kollie's family, fled their country with their many resources and talents. After the war, Liberia became an economic wasteland where 85 percent of the population is unemployed and impoverished, much like America's inner-cities, where businesses, resources, and talents have also fled. Kollie's mission has become a journey to rebuild his beloved country by nobly entering into the pain to reconcile the broken spiritual and economical relationships, as is being done at Bridge.

Kollie and I discussed family life in Liberia and their economy before the Civil War. From his perspective, before the civil war they had whole families and a rather good economy. People worked and families raised their children. Life was basically good before the civil war. I told Kollie that the fact that the Liberian culture had a remembrance of what whole families and economic wellbeing looked like was most important. I told him that over a few generations this remembrance has become especially forgotten in our impoverished inner-city neighborhoods of America today.

I asked him about troubled youth. He said that they didn't have many problems with their children, because "our children listen." He thought and then said, "except for those children who lost their fathers in the civil war. We do have issues with our fatherless youth." I told him that 98 percent of our children at Bridge were fatherless, and their moms (like widows) were probably the loneliest people in America. Also along with our high illegitimacy rates, I told him about the increasing high divorce rate in America and how fatherlessness and broken homes are a growing and untested social experiment that first-world America has not yet fully experienced the consequences of.

I asked Kollie about their children's respect and thankfulness. He quickly said, "that is not a problem in Liberia. Our children are very respectful and thankful." He said that respect is a strong and deep cultural value. I told Kollie that, as a culture, America has become more disrespectful since the early 1960's. Today in our inner-cities our children can hear their peers' silent body language, but many times will not hear the audible voice of adults.

Ten years ago our Bridge neighbors told us that the neighborhood children on the streets were disrespectful and ungrateful. Our older neighborhood residents have told us that respect and thankfulness were a much higher value in Bridge's neighborhood 50 years ago. They have told us, "This is a different world now." (Note: Some authors call our inner-cities of America, "The Fourth World." The fourth world refers to our undeveloped and disconnected inner-cities within first-world America.)

Mother Teresa once said that a human's greatest needs are "to be loved and to love." I would add to this quote "to be respected and to respect." When a child is treated as a throwaway by society (i.e., disrespect of human dignity), they learn to expect to see "the face" of disrespect from others when they enter any room. The children from generational poverty know this "face" and return it well. We simply reap what we sow (Gal 6:7b, paraphrased).

At the end of our visit, Kollie encouragingly told us that if he lived in America he would work at the Bridge. I found this intriguing and bonding when this man from third-world Africa visiting first-world America so quickly and clearly heard America's fourth world calling him according to God's Will! Thank you Kollie, you are a true repairer and restorer of broken foundations.

"Those from among you Shall build the old waste places;
You shall raise up the foundations of many generations;
And you shall be called the Repairer of the Breach,
The Restorer of Streets to Dwell In." (Isa 58:12, NKJV)

12/04/2013

A BOY AND A MAN

"Young people take pride in their strength, but the gray hairs of wisdom are even more beautiful."
(Proverbs 20:29, CEV)

In 2009, Bridge's Boy Scout masters, Dan Pierce and Ron Czarnecki, took the boys on a camp-out at Bill and Mary Langford's Cherokee Horse Farm.

Bill taught the scouts about an animal's "fight or flight" response to perceived danger, and how horses usually respond to danger by flight. It is a primitive, automatic, inborn response to insure their survival. A horse is very sensitive to human body language due to the flight instinct. Understanding this helps a person learn to better communicate with and gain a horse's trust.

The scouts then learned how to ride and direct horses without confusing them with mixed body signals and rein control. Some of the guys caught on quickly, while others confused the horses to the point that the horse would not respond at all. They all had fun, except perhaps one horse.

Early the next morning after pond fishing, one of the boys declared that he could beat Dan in a foot race. Without hesitation, Dan said, "See that tree out there, we'll race to it and back." The boy immediately said he was going to "beat him bad."

I quickly estimated the distance to the tree and back to be almost a mile. I was taken aback by this long distance challenge from a fifty-four year old man. In any case, the challenge was accepted. They stripped down to their boxer shorts and sock feet, and I noticed that whatever Dan did, the boy did also.

The race was on! They were fairly even out to the tree as far as we could tell. Dan grabbed a leaf and made the turn, yet the young scout stayed behind. We thought the boy was giving the old man a head start as the boy began sprinting after Dan. About half way back it happened. The boy stopped, gasped for air, and went to his knees. He finally straightened up and began walking as Dan crossed the finish line. We congratulated the tired man, and began yelling encouragement to the boy to continue running and finish his race. He did. Entering and finishing his race is a win in itself for the boy.

The old man's win was decisive, but the main win was that the man gained the young scout's respect while the young boy gained a piece of the man's wisdom. As the man knew up front, the race will be won not by short-term speed of the boy, but by the good and long-term pace of the old man. It is through respect of each other that good things happen. When an admiring man stands alongside a younger boy encouraging him "up" and not "down," something good always rubs off for both.

A young boy's glory is his strength, while an old man's glory is his wisdom. In their earned mutual respect, the old man could then pour his hard won wisdom into a young boy's life. On that Sunday morning, they all stopped, sat under large live oaks by a pond and reflected on God's Word and His awesome creation of which we are all a part. And all the boys listened to the men. We are all worthy and thankful to be a part of this beautiful world at this specific time together while living in love and respect of God and each other.

I look back on my life and thank God for crusty wise old men like Dan, and feel sad knowing that many young boys and girls will never rub shoulders with these authentic, capable and caring men who, along with wisdom, are becoming extinct in our culture today. It leaves a hole in a child's soul not to have an admiring and wise man in their life. It is a hole that many men try to fill with various "flight or fight" addictions that do not work.

We respect Dan and Ron as quiet heroes who have given three years of their lives to come to the Bridge Ministry of Acadiana to share their lives with our young scouts. (Note: Troop #915 is the only troop in the Evangeline Area Council established by men who are not the fathers of their scouts.)

The Bridge also thanks great heroes like Bill and Mary Langford for continually sharing their resources and prayers with our under-resourced children and neighborhood. We also thank the Boy Scouts of America that have helped raise many boys into fine gentlemen. It does not take just any old village to raise a child, but a Beloved Community that respects and loves God, self, and all people.

"My son, pay attention to my wisdom. Open your ears to my understanding; so that you may act with foresight and speak with insight.
(Proverbs 5:1-2, GW)

02/03/2014

GIRL DRAMA

by Erin Greneaux
Bridge Elementary Youth Director

With almost half of our elementary program consisting of 4th-5th graders, you can be sure we deal with a lot of attitudes and our fair share of "girl drama." It only takes one look exchanged between two 5th grade girls to start some whispering in the corner, a few "accidental" shoves when moving between groups, and finally all-out war with everyone picking sides and arguing.

We have tried so many things, but these girls seem to hold on to grudges and anger more than anyone. Two of our girls in particular could no longer be in the same room with each other. I finally gave what was really an empty threat—if there was any more disrespect between them, they would be each other's new partner in every activity for the rest of the year. They were horrified, but I guarantee I wanted to deal with that arrangement even less that they did!

The inevitable happened, and when they threatened to hit each other one day, we started a new group—the two girls and myself. The first day we did writing assignments. One would read a writing prompt and answer out loud, while the other would write down the dictated answer and read it back, and then they would alternate. They used every bit of body language possible to show their disdain for each other until I called parents to pick them up. I let them know that we would be in our special group the next day, and if they couldn't deal with it, they would have to stay home.

The second day, we repeated the process. It was so painfully awkward to watch them express their dislike of one another for no reason except pride. The third day, one of the girls came with a changed attitude, ready to work and learn and ignore the other girl. While she took the high road, the other one took on an even worse attitude. I pulled her aside to tell her that treating a person like a disease was unacceptable behavior and that if Jesus died for us while we were still sinners, so she could manage to forgive this girl and treat her as a child of God. When I told her she would have to go home for the way she had acted, she broke down crying. I called her mom to pick her up, but there was no answer, so I had no choice but to go back to our lovely group of three and continue the lesson.

Amazingly, after our talk, the girl's attitude was completely changed. She participated in the activity and stopped her vengeful behavior. When she was finally picked up at the end of the day, she asked me if she could come back the next day and promised that she would participate. I told her she could come the next day and I would hold her to it (and told her mom to be ready to pick her up).

The next day I put the two girls together to read a book out loud to each other, but couldn't sit with them as other children needed help on an assignment. They read to each other the entire time, taking turns, without arguing, and even helping each other on difficult to pronounce words. This may seem like a small accomplishment to anyone on the outside, but all of the kids at Bridge recognized the change.

One boy commented, "Are they friends now? I thought they hated each other!" This is the first step in a long process, but this is what Bridge is all about—bridging gaps between people and, in the process, showing them how to bridge the gap between us and God. One day at a time, one step closer, we are using Christ as an example to show what "success" in life looks like—a life that reflects Christ's character.

"...In love. Make every effort to keep the unity of the Spirit through the bond of peace." (Ephesians 4:2b-3, NIV)

02/21/2014

GRIT

"Quitters Never Win & Winners Never Quit"
(Vince Lombardi)

By An Anonymous
Bridge Volunteer and Business Owner

In our math tutoring game yesterday at Bridge one of my three 3rd graders, Sam, lagged behind. It became apparent to him that he could not keep up with the others and that he would lose that particular game. I was very impressed with how Sam adjusted to the situation as he kept his head up and continued to participate throughout the entire game with the same positive spirit and attitude he displayed when the game first began. I was very much inspired by this young fellow.

Tutoring Sam made me reflect on my past struggles through the years of school, college, early work, marriage, children, and starting a new business. Reflecting on those early years in our business, I remembered being in a dog-eat-dog mode where our newly formed, unknown company was basically picking up scraps the other consultants dropped on the floor. After the first couple years and constant 12-hour workdays, I developed an attitude of prideful self-pity and was very much upset that we could not land a certain big client. I passionately felt that our company offered the best service at the best price and would always work for our client's business as if it were our own.

"Why were we not able to land that big client and firmly establish our business?" At the point of giving up, my partner advised me to continue to work hard and have faith that all will work out for the good. At that time I needed his gritty encouragement to stay in the game.

And I did stay in the game and things have worked out very well for our company. After landing the client that I wanted and many others, I soon realized that God had a plan for our business and for me. I soon realized that if we would have landed that big client in the first few years, we probably would not have been able to keep up with the volume of work, thereby possibly destroying our young company.

I also realize, from a deeper perspective, that God has a plan for young Sam and us all—that we just have to passionately train, work hard, do our best, and then within God's will have the faith to "let go and let God." Now being under God's schedule, I am able to fully recognize and am grateful for all His blessings that I can now share with others like Sam. I know now that the things I once viewed as so critical are merely training bumps in the road that will build a little bit more of Christ's character in me and lead to His greater destiny. Under my old narrow schedule, none of these true blessings would have been recognized.

Recently about 25 Bridge children, along with Sam, were encouraged by Bridge staff to participate in a musical the Bridge produced. This musical required a commitment from our children and Sam. This was a commitment that set high expectations; many practice sessions, memorizations, dancing, singing and, of course, a scheduled grand performance that my wife and I attended. They committed themselves to the task, they did not quit, and they were pleased with doing their job successfully under pressure. Stretching our children in new ways develops true grit. Grit that Sam exhibited that day in tutoring.

Grit is a learned and developed character skill and trait. Grit is considered a major factor in determining success and happiness in life. Studying grit and reflecting deeper with a friend of mine about grit, we found some of the building blocks that develop the habits of grit in us to be: passion, setting and committing to long term tasks and goals, accepting the challenge of higher expectations, willingly working hard, learning self-control in spite of one's feelings, positive thinking, delayed gratification, focus, and practice, practice, practice, and seeing the task finished to the end without ever quitting.

In our grit discussions my friend and I also discussed our own role models in life who were most important in the development of this character trait. Our role models were capable and caring people who encouraged us without doing for us what we were designed to do for ourselves. We also remembered that our role models were very close to us and knew us well. We felt admired and loved by them. They stretched us. They would not allow us to quit, while expecting the best from us. They encouraged us to push through our discomforts and humiliations and taught us the Way. By knowing us, they never gave us more than we could bear up under.

We came to believe in ourselves, only because our

role models first believed in us and loved us first, and they were there, and never gave up on us. Our beloved encouragers never "fixed" our struggles for us, but wisely "embraced" our struggle alongside us. They seemed to love our struggles and taught us to love them too. For they knew that it is most important for a person to deal with their struggles and overcome them and finally say, "I did it myself!" They encouraged us to try many new things that empowered us to say, "I can do that too!" They taught us how to win.

Children, especially in our inner-cities, require adults in their life daily who admire, love, encourage, and believe in them for a long enough time for them to finally believe in themselves and become able and eager to do for themselves. They need adults to encourage them never to cave in and quit, but to passionately stay in the game of life to succeed.

Since meeting Sam at Bridge, I can say that he has in me one more gritty admirer and believer! Please do not give up praying for all our Bridge children.

"We also glory in our sufferings, because we know that suffering produces perseverance; perseverance, character; and character, hope." (Romans 5:3-4, NIV)

04/08/2014

THE SHAFT OF LIGHT

"The Word became flesh and blood,
and moved into the neighborhood."
(John 1:14a, MSG)

Ironically it all began in the humble setting of a lowly, dingy, smelly animal stall. A child is born. In that instance a shaft of light splits our darkness. The Light of the World becomes flesh and moves into our neighborhood, physically sent to show us the Way.

He physically entered our world because of His great love for all His creation, which includes you and me. Motivated by this love, He modeled for us up-close and personally how to love our Father, others, and even ourselves. This is Good News.

Jesus entered into our broken world in grace and truth to reconcile our broken relationships with God, self, neighbor, and creation; and, to redeem the wholeness that He designed for us to have so long ago, individually and collectively. He modeled right relationships, and the right way to think, care, and act. He showed us how these right ways are built upon His grace and truth. This is Good News.

Jesus lovingly moved in and lived among us. Our problems became His problems. Our pain became His pain. Our brokenness became His brokenness. Our pride became His ultimate sacrifice. Amazing grace. Within His New Covenant promises He is our God that has forever freed those who trust Him from sin. We are His people and He will always be with us and "in" us along with His word. This is Great News! Powerful news indeed.

Jesus then prayed "(Father) just as you sent Me into the world, I also have sent them into the world" (John 17:18, AMP). Jesus is Bridge Ministry of Acadiana's much-needed model of development and empowerment. Jesus relocated, reconciled, and redeemed (3-R's of Development). As Jesus moved into our neighborhood, we have humbly relocated into the Bridge neighborhood to reconcile broken relationships and redeem our (spiritual and physical) wholeness, individually and collectively. Becoming the living proof of a loving God in a hurting and broken Lafayette neighborhood. Becoming His shaft of Light.

At Bridge we thank God for you and your family! May the Good News of Christ's birth bring forth Light, Love, Joy, and Peace in your life. We love you and our community! Merry Christmas from Bridge Ministry of Acadiana!

"Thy kingdom come, thy will be done on earth …."
(Matthew 6:10a, KJV)

THE SEEDS OF FRIENDSHIPS

"Anyone can count the seeds in an apple,
But only God can count the apples in a seed."
(Robert Schuller)

By Jennifer Reynaud, Executive Director

About six months ago I met a neighborhood lady who was out walking her dog. For anonymity purposes I will call her Sadie. Our conversations in the beginning were about her dog and dog training tips. We eventually got to the topic of Bridge, and I invited Sadie to attend the upcoming Neighborhood Association meeting and or our Adult Bible study on Monday nights.

Since that time, Sadie has been attending all the Neighborhood and Bible Study meetings. At these meetings, she has been quietly thankful for being received with the open arms of her new friends and neighbors.

A few months ago, she came to our new children's building to deliver an envelope. I curiously opened it and to my humble surprise it was a donation to the Bridge along with a note telling us "thank you." She told me to use the money as the ministry needed because she had been blessed by Bridge Ministry. I let her know that I would put it in our Building Fund because we were close to finishing a most generous matching-fund campaign for Phase I, AND that her investment would be instantly doubled! Her eyes lit up with excitement knowing that she was partnering with us on a higher level.

Recently, Sadie told me that she had some legal issues with her home loan. Her loan agreement seemed to have some restrictive clauses that she did not understand. Tom, a lawyer who is a Bridge volunteer and investor, had offered to sit down with our neighbors, so Sadie gave him a call about her situation. As it turned out, they were able to clear up the issues, which freed her to make future improvement decisions on her own home. (Thank You Tom for sharing your gifts. For a neighborhood used to apathy, you choosing to be their friend is most empowering!)

While Sadie continues to be a part of the Neighborhood Association and Adult Bible study, she has also begun attending Bridge's Adult Exercise Group. Plus, with the encouragement of her neighbors, she has joined one of the neighborhood leadership teams that are planning the neighborhood events for the fall season. *"As iron sharpens iron, so a friend sharpens a friend." (Proverbs 27:17 NLT)*

Sadie is just one example of a life that is changing through the power of friendships, and becoming a life that is breathing life into others. Real change is not usually done by some apparent great action, but simply by starting a friendly conversation that invites others "in," willingly walks through life's struggles together as friends, and intends to leave God's good creation better because of it all.

At Bridge we have experienced that as our loving friendships with God and neighbors increase, crime decreases; and, our children begin to feel safer and more secure. As safety and security slowly increase, the seeds of belonging and caring begin to build us all up (including our children's attitudes and grades). It is truly a joy to visibly see these seeds of friendships that will naturally build up shalom in our city, in our families, and in us.

"Seek the shalom of the city where I have sent you,
For in its shalom, you will find your shalom."
(Rephrased from Jeremiah 29:7)

08/13/2013

JOY

By an Anonymous Bridge Volunteer

I think that while on this earth, God lovingly acts on our behalf through other people. While I have had more heart aches and pain in my lifetime than I sometimes thought I could bear, God has repeatedly let me know that through others He has been with me the whole way.

I recently celebrated my 70th birthday with the realization that there is more joy in my life now than at any time in the past. As a result, I spend almost all my prayer time and quiet time reflecting on God's blessings in my life and thanking Him. The Bible says, "*Be still and know that I am God.*" *(Psalm 46:10a, NIV)*

This joy has not often been the case in my past. When I was five years old, my father died at age 32 of a massive heart attack. In those days there were no day cares or aftercare facilities like there are today. My younger sister and I were placed in one boarding house after another. I will not go into detail, but they were akin to the descriptions of such places found in Dicken's novel *Oliver Twist.* The reason we were placed in several different homes (while my mother tried to make a living cleaning offices) was because I would often take my sister by the hand, and we would run away. In our running, we were always seeking the home of our maternal grandmother and grandfather.

Having the luxury of reflecting back now I see how God helped me through the pain of childhood by providing wise and wonderful grandparents for my sister and myself. I know firsthand that, for a boy, growing up without a father is like trying to live with no direction or guidance at all. Like a sailboat without a rudder, a boy will drift aimlessly and without direction. But God's provision for me was to provide a substitute in my grandparents. Until rather late in my adult life, they were the guidance and evidence of God's love for me.

In 1968, I was sent to Vietnam as a platoon leader in the Central Highlands. At age 24 my job was to lead a group of 30 men to remove booby-traps from the bridges blown up by the enemy, and then rebuild the bridges. Once again, God's protection was revealed in my life in the midst of war. I never expected to come home alive. My prayer, repeated over and over on the plane to Vietnam, was that I was ready to die if it was God's will, but that I did not want to be the cause of the death of any of the men entrusted to my care.

Miraculously, only three of my men were wounded in the 14 months that I served. None were killed. There were numerous times in which I thought I would be killed as we embarked on dangerous missions. One day my Jeep hit a landmine that blew it to smithereens. None of the men riding with me were injured, as we were all thrown free from the exploding Jeep. All I received was a bruised and cut up knee. Two weeks before, my other men had taken my Jeep to the motor pool and welded a 2 inch steel floor in my Jeep and placed two layers of sandbags over the steel. The weight was enormous, but the men assured me that even though I would have to drive slower, the steel protection would keep me from being killed. God's people were protecting my men and me.

On another occasion, as a duty officer, I ran to my perimeter guard tower to direct return fire from an attack. The next day, my men took me to the place where I was running and showed me over 100 bullet holes in the wall alongside my path. I never knew that I was even being shot at! God had answered my prayer, but more importantly, He let me know that He had plans for my life. However I did not fully realize that fact until later in life, much later.

After returning home from the war, I became an angry and bitter man. I drank way too much alcohol, ruined two marriages, and had four children that I did not have a clue how to raise. After about 15 years of such lunacy, I had destroyed all relationships in my life except that of my grandparents, and yet God blessed me still again. To this day I am profoundly grateful and perplexed that God would give me another chance. But He did. He sent Anita to share and be part of my life.

For the past 27 years, she has been the greatest blessing God has given me. She is a true Proverbs 31 woman. And, as with all marriages, you not only get a wife, you also get her family. That can be a blessing or a curse. In my case it was an enormous blessing because JW Benson walked into my life. Anita's daddy was the most humble, godly, Christian man and father that I had ever met. The first years of our marriage, I simply watched his example and decided that I wanted to have a family like his and to be a man of God like him. I returned to my first love, God, by worshiping and serving Him. I went to Promise Keepers conference and took my three sons, who all professed their faith in Jesus Christ.

My relationships with my children flourished. I am blessed with nine grandchildren. These are my crowns.

God also provided me with spiritual gifts and talents, which my pastor has been discussing lately. I took the spiritual gifts test and was mildly surprised that my number one spiritual gift is faith. In remembering my past, I can now see how His seed of faith planted in me has grown. My faith is the greatest gift that God has given me. It has nurtured and sustained me for most of my life. As to talents, God gave me a good intellect and the ability to advocate for other people in need. Hence, through hard work and determination, I became a lawyer. I thank God every day for the abilities He has given me. All my professional dreams and aspirations have been fulfilled in practicing law.

My pastor often asks me what God is revealing to me these days. The last several years God has let me know through His word that He loves me and has blessed me greatly, and that He now invites me, calls me, to bless others.

I serve as a volunteer at Bridge Ministry of Acadiana. I see the young fatherless children at the Bridge as a reflection of myself as an angry young man without direction. Most of the middle school kids at the Bridge are just like I was, but I let them know that God, our Father, will never give up on them. If God did it for me, He will do it for them because His very nature is unconditional love. The Bridge is truly a special place for them.

I also share with you today the sheer joy I now have in life. We continue to have struggles and difficulties like all families, but I know without a single doubt that God is "for" me as He is "for" you too. I recently attended the wedding of the daughter of a very good friend. The priest who performed the ceremony quoted an Australian minister who said: "Joy is that infallible sign of the presence of God."

I love that and know that our Father's joyful presence is a gift that is here today and will be here for all our tomorrows.

"You turned my wailing into dancing;
you removed my sackcloth and clothed me with joy"
(Psalm 30:11, NIV)

06/15/2014

Recommended Reading List

- Theirs is the Kingdom by Robert D. Lupton
- Toxic Charity: How Churches and Charities Hurt Those They Help (And How To Reverse It) by Robert Lupton.
- A Quiet Revolution by John Perkins.
- Making Neighborhoods Whole: A Handbook for Christian Community Development by John M. Perkins
- When Helping Hurts by Steve Corbett and Brian Fikkert.
- Building a People of Power by Robert Linthicum.
- Compassion, Justice and the Christian Life: Rethinking Ministry to the Poor (Aka, "And You Call Yourself a Christian, toward responsibly charity") by Robert Lupton.
- With Justice for All by John Perkins.
- Beyond Charity by John M. Perkins.
- Breaking Down Walls: A Model for Reconciliation in an Age of Racial Strife by Glen Kehrein and Raleigh Washington.
- From Oppression to Jubilee Justice by Lowell Noble.
- The Next Evangelicalism, Freeing the Church from Western Cultural Captivity by Soong-Chan Rah. 2010

- A Framework for Understanding Poverty by Ruby K. Payne
- Doing Faithjustice by Fred Kammer, S.J.
- Christianity and the Social Crisis by Walter Rauschenbusch.
- Divided by Faith by Emerson and Smith
- The Church of Irresistible Influence by Robert Lewis
- Bowling Alone, the Collapse and Revival of American Community by Robert D. Putnam.
- Kingdom Calling by Amy Sherman.
- The Treasure Principle by Randy Alcorn.
- Wealth Conundrum by Ralph Doudera.
- Four Pillars of a Man's Heart by Stu Weber.
- Bringing Up Boys by Dr. James Dobson.

"**God's Purpose** *in all this was to use the Church to display his wisdom in its rich variety to all the unseen rulers and authorities in the heavenly places. 11 This was his eternal plan, which he carried out through Christ Jesus our Lord." (Ephesians 3:10-11, NLT)*

THE BRIDGE MINISTRY OF ACADIANA, INC. is an Inner-City Development Mission (not Relief) with the Philosophy to:

Go to the People
Live among them,
Learn from them,
Love them.
Start with what they know,
Build with what they have,
But with the best of leaders,
When their task is done,
The People will remark:
"We Have Done It Ourselves!"

Bridge's "8 KEYS" of Christian Community Development (www.ccda.org) are:

1. Relocate. The Bridge moved into the 4-Corner's neighborhood as Jesus humbly and lovingly moved into our neighborhood.
2. Reconcile. Bridge participants are God's Ambassadors of Reconciliation. Bridge believes that poverty is caused by our 3-broken relationships with God, self(s), and neighbors. Herein, it is God's Will to lovingly reconcile these 3-relationships, so that God's blessing can rightly and justly flows vertically and horizontally.
3. Redeem. Bridge's goal is God's goal to redeem what has been lost of the Kingdom in our world spiritually and economically.
4. Listen to the Neighborhood
5. Develop Indigenous Leadership

6. Christ Centered
7. Approach Development Wholistically
8. Empowerment/Development (not 'relief').

These '8 Keys' of Bridge's Christian Community Development within Jesus' Greatest Commandments are the principles that underlie and direct Bridge Ministry of Acadiana's many relational programs and activities alongside our children, adults, neighborhood and our community of Bridge builders. All relational programming is designed as a multifaceted comprehensive system that develops God's character and wholeness in people on both sides of the 'bridge'.

Proceeds from the Sale of this book go to:

Bridge Ministry of Acadiana, Inc.

Jennifer Reynaud, Executive Director
337-235-6565
P.O. Box 62029, Lafayette, Louisiana 70596
www.bridgeacadiana.org
(Located at 512 North University,
Lafayette, Louisiana 70501)

**THREE WAYS TO JOIN
THE BRIDGE REVOLUTION:
Pray-Volunteer-Invest**

CPSIA information can be obtained at www.ICGtesting.com
Printed in the USA
LVOW11s0808220115

423789LV00001B/2/P

9 781462 755967